GEORGE WASHINGTON, ENTREPRENEUR

ALSO BY JOHN BERLAU

Eco-Freaks

GEORGE WASHINGTON, ENTREPRENEUR

How Our Founding Father's
Private Business Pursuits Changed
America and the World

JOHN BERLAU

ALL
POINTS
BOOKS

NEW YORK

First published in the United States by All Points Books, an imprint of St. Martin's Publishing Group

www.allpointsbooks.com

Designed by Meryl Sussman Levavi

Library of Congress Cataloging-in-Publication Data

Names: Berlau, John, 1971– author.
Title: George Washington, entrepreneur : how our founding father's private
    business pursuits changed America and the world / John Berlau.
Other titles: How our founding father's private business pursuits changed
    America and the world
Description: First edition. | New York : All Points Books, 2020. | Includes
    bibliographical references and index.
Identifiers: LCCN 2019058376 | ISBN 9781250172600 (hardcover) |
    ISBN 9781250172617 (ebook)
Subjects: LCSH: Washington, George, 1732-1799—Career in business. |
    Businesspeople—United States—Biography. | Entrepreneurship—
    Virginia—Mount Vernon (Estate)—History—18th century. | Mount
    Vernon (Va. : Estate)—Biography.
Classification: LCC HC102.5.W375 B47 2020 | DDC 338/.04092 [B]—dc23
LC record available at https://lccn.loc.gov/2019058376

First Edition: 2020

10 9 8 7 6 5 4 3 2 1

DEDICATION

I dedicate this book to the memory of my father, Harry Litman Berlau, who cheered on this book—as he did my every endeavor—but didn't live to see it released for publication. Dad, you taught me the value of history, wise investment, and fair dealing. You provided a strong roof for our family and lots of love and laughter under that roof for me, my sister, and our wonderful mom. Dad, you may have left this earth on May 6, 2019, but you'll always be with me!

CONTENTS

✦➝⊜⊑➝✦

A NOTE ON SPELLING

◦→⟐◦ ◦⟐←◦

I believe there is value in quoting George Washington, and other historical figures, in their own words as much as possible. Thus, I let Washington and his contemporaries speak for themselves quite a bit by quoting passages from their speeches, letters, and diary entries that I believe readers can understand with relative ease. However, there may still be a slight barrier with regard to spelling conventions in eighteenth-century America.

At the time, there was no standardized spelling across the colonies or even within them. American English gradually became standardized in the early nineteenth century after an educational entrepreneur named Noah Webster began publishing spelling books and his famous dictionary, which continues today as *The Merriam-Webster Dictionary*. A strong supporter of the American Revolution, Webster believed that unification of the language was necessary for unity in the new country.[1]

In some instances, I will note in brackets spelling and

grammar that I believe may be distracting or confusing. At other times, I will just let the documents speak, as I do not wish my voice to become a distraction. I thank the reader in advance for bearing with me in my attempt to bring the voices of Washington and his contemporaries to light.

INTRODUCTION

✦

WASHINGTON'S GREENHOUSE

The Mount Vernon Greenhouse as Reconstructed at Mount Vernon

It was August of 1784, and George Washington had many things on his mind.

He was once again a private citizen, having retired from his position as general six months earlier, after eight years of holding together the ragtag Continental Army and leading it to victory in the Revolutionary War. But he was troubled by the emerging problems of monetary instability in the new nation and its lack of an adequate defense from foreign aggressors. These issues and others would lead him to accept—reluctantly—the nomination to be the first president of the United States some five years later.

But a prime focus of his mind this month had been a more appetizing thought—a plan to grow the then-exotic fruits of oranges, lemons, limes, and others of the citrus variety. Washington had possessed a love of citrus fruits ever since he traveled to Barbados—in what would be his only trip out of the North American continent—at the age of 19 in 1751.

Traveling with his older brother in the hopes that the warm tropical weather would improve Lawrence's ailing health, the young Washington wrote in his diary of the "many delicious fruits" he had tasted. These included pears, oranges, and pineapples, the latter of which became Washington's favorite island fruit. "None pleases my taste as do's [sic] the pine," Washington wrote.[1] Washington's business records show that decades later he would frequently order citrus fruits and "a few pine apples" (in his words) from shippers who carried goods to and from the Caribbean.[2]

Washington had long wanted to grow these fruits at Mount Vernon, the Northern Virginia farm and estate on which he had lived—off and on—ever since he was a teenager. He knew these crops would not survive the Northern Virginia winters. Over the last few years, however, Washington had read and heard about an agricultural innovation called a "greenhouse" in which these tropical fruits could be grown in environmentally controlled conditions.

The idea of manipulating temperature to grow nonnative crops was not new. In ancient Rome, plants were moved in and out of the sunlight to grow certain fruits and vegetables for the emperor Tiberius.[3] In the sixteenth century, separate buildings to house plants and insulate them from rough weather began to be erected by royalty and aristocracy in England and the Netherlands.[4] By the mid-eighteenth century, as technology had made better quality glass more widely available for construction, the royal families and landed gentry erected greenhouses on the grounds of many of Europe's palaces and estates.[5] Possession of a greenhouse, according to gardening historian Mac Griswold, implied that a landowner had "scaled the heights of power and fashion."[6]

But in the new American republic, in contrast to the nations of old Europe, greenhouses were still few and far between. A handful of greenhouses had been built, including the one constructed in Boston around the 1730s by the Faneuils, a wealthy family of merchants who would later donate to Boston the still-standing Faneuil Hall market and meeting place.[7] However, no greenhouses had been constructed in Northern Virginia, and none of Washington's friends and neighbors knew how to build one.

Whenever Washington found local knowledge limited he would reach beyond his immediate circle. In this case, he did not have to travel far—only to the neighboring state of Maryland—where there existed a famous greenhouse at Mount Clare, a grand estate in Baltimore that belonged to members of the prominent Carroll family.

Though geographically close, the Carrolls of Maryland were culturally quite a distance away from the Virginia families with whom George and Martha Washington typically rubbed elbows. Irish-Catholics like the Carrolls had fled to America to escape persecution in Great Britain but faced similar prejudice from colonists of English ancestry. In most of the colonies, Catholics couldn't hold public office, and in Virginia they couldn't even pray publicly.[8]

But neither Catholics nor other religious minorities faced any prejudice from George Washington. Washington had learned on the battlefield to work with people from all walks of life. Several of Washington's officers were Irish, including Colonel John Fitzgerald, who served as one of his top aides. Fitzgerald would be a co-founder after the war of Virginia's first Catholic parish, the St. Mary's congregation in Alexandria, which continues to this day and was granted "basilica" status by the Vatican in 2018 due to its historic roots.

Washington had begun his friendship with members

of the Carroll family almost a decade earlier. In 1775, Charles Carroll, who would the next year become the sole Catholic signer of the Declaration of Independence and later one of Maryland's first U.S. senators, informed Washington of an agricultural pamphlet that described what he believed to be the "most advantageous method of cultivating & preparing hemp."[9] The two men would continue to correspond about agriculture, military strategy, and politics until Washington's death in 1799.

Now it was the widow of Carroll's cousin—an attorney also named Charles who was commonly referred to as "Charles Carroll, Barrister" to avoid confusion—with whom Washington wished to speak. He and his wife Margaret had become known for the succulent fruits and vegetables they grew in the fields of Mount Clare and in their greenhouse. When Charles died in 1783, Margaret continued to run an efficient operation and even expanded the types of plants at the greenhouse.

In 1784, Washington wrote to Margaret's brother-in-law Tench Tilghman, who had served as one of Washington's top aides during the Revolutionary War, seeking detailed information about the construction of Mrs. Carroll's greenhouse. The letter conveys Washington's passion for the project and amply displays the technical turn of his mind.[10]

Dear Sir,

I shall essay the finishing of my Green Ho. [greenhouse] this fall; but find that neither my own knowledge, or that of any person abt me, is competent to the business.

Shall I, for this reason, ask the favor of you to give me a short detail of the internal construction of the Green House at Mrs Carrolls?

I am perswaded *now,* that I planned mine upon too contracted a Scale—My House is (of Brick) 40 feet by 24 in the outer dimensions—& half the width is disposed of for two rooms back of the part designed for the Green House; leaving not more than about 37 by 10 in the clear for the latter. As there is no cover on the walls yet, I can raise them to any height.

The information I wish to receive is on the following points.

The dimensions of Mrs Carrolls Green House?

What kind of a floor is to it?

How high from *that* floor to the bottom of the Window frame?

What height the Windows are from bottom to top?

How high from the top to the Cieling?

Whether the Cieling is flat? or of what kind?

Whether the heat is conveyed by flues and a grate?

Whether the grate is on the out, or inside?

Whether the Flues run all round the House?

The size of them without, and in the hollow?

Whether they join the Wall, or are seperate from it?

If the latter, how far are they apart?

With any other suggestions which you may conceive it necessary to give.

I should be glad to hear from you on this subject soon, as I shall leave home on or before the first of Next Month on a journey to the Westward, and wish to give particular directions to the workmen before I go.

I hope you will excuse the trouble the solution of these enquiries will occasion. I am—Dr Sir Yr most Obedt Hble Servt

> Go: Washington

Tilghman answered these questions as best he could, but shortly thereafter Margaret Carroll herself took over the correspondence, and a lovely friendship was struck as letters went back and forth from Washington to the widow Carroll for more than five years. At a time when it was unusual for a man to take business advice from a woman who was not immediate family, Washington addresses Carroll with the admiration of an eager student seeking to learn everything he can from someone whom he readily concedes has more knowledge on the subject.

When Carroll offered Washington plants for his newly built greenhouse, he eagerly accepted, though he was adamant she not incur any extra expense on his account. "I am desirous to profit of the very obliging offer you were pleased some time ago to make me," Washington wrote in September 1789. "In availing myself of your goodness I am far from desiring that it should induce any inconvenience to yourself—but, reconciling your disposition to oblige, with your convenience, I shall be happy to receive such aids as you can well spare, and as will not impair your collection." Washington signed the letter affectionately, "your obliged and obedient servant."[11]

Hardly anything in this letter gives an indication that its author was anything more than a very entrepreneurial farmer. Yet when he wrote it, he had already been serving as the first U.S. president for more than four months.

These letters to Tilghman and Carroll weren't unique. Washington wrote detailed, sometimes passionate, letters about agriculture his entire life, and they did not cease on the battlefield or during his presidency. As historian Joseph J. Ellis writes in *His Excellency: George Washington*: "The longest letters, and more of them than he devoted to any official topic, deal with the management of his farms at Mount Vernon. Even when immersed in crucial diplomatic negotiations with France or controversial deliberations about Hamilton's fiscal policy, Washington found time to compose meticulous instructions to his managers about plowing, weeding, worming, or grubbing schedules."[12]

The gifts from Mrs. Carroll arrived by boat at Mount Vernon near the end of 1789. She had sent a variety of plants, including some small trees that had to be transplanted into the Mount Vernon greenhouse. There were nine lemon trees and nine orange trees, two grapefruit trees that were in the eighteenth century called "shaddocks," and aloe and marjoram herbs that even today are considered exotic plants in the United States.[13] In addition, Washington would also grow in the greenhouse lime trees, coffee plants, and a sago palm tree from India.[14]

Guests at Mount Vernon, including European dignitaries, would marvel at the greenhouse and the gallery of plants inside it. A clergyman from Pennsylvania who visited Mount Vernon in 1799 wrote of seeing "a great variety of plants and flowers, wonderful in appearance, exquisite in their perfume and delightful to the eye."[15] A French visitor in 1792 wrote that the greenhouse and

Mount Vernon itself projected "an elegant and majestic simplicity."[16]

"An elegant and majestic simplicity." At first, the phrase seems contradictory. But upon reflection, the phrase encapsulates the perfect description of innovation. It can also describe the dynamic process of enriching oneself by benefitting others—identified by Adam Smith as the "invisible hand" of capitalism.

Adjectives like "creative" and "innovative" at first don't seem to apply to Washington as much as other founding fathers like Jefferson and Franklin. In reality, Washington was just as creative as they were. But his creativity was of a different type. Whereas Franklin built gadgets at his homestead, and Jefferson designed fancy buildings, Washington built a series of interconnected businesses.

Over the past decade, a group of scholars and those who administer the Mount Vernon Estate and Gardens have begun to celebrate Washington's private pursuits. In *The Unexpected George Washington,* Harlow Giles Unger notes that Washington was "one of America's leading entrepreneurs" who "expanded a relatively small tobacco plantation into a diversified agroindustrial enterprise."[17] Historian Edward Lengel writes that "Washington was a crafty and diligent entrepreneur . . . His personal experiences and abilities as an entrepreneur inspired his policies as general and president."[18]

And more than most of the founding fathers, Washington can hold the title of "self-made man." Washington's background wasn't exactly poor, but it was not as rich as many of his contemporaries among the founders.

His father died when he was 11, and, having two older half-brothers, he didn't inherit much, and the family lacked money to give him a formal education.

Yet Washington constantly sought to learn. As he did with Mrs. Carroll, he would habitually seek out experts in certain fields and pepper them—politely—with questions. Historian Kevin J. Hayes, whose research shows that Washington was much more of a reader than previous historians have given him credit for, points out that Washington approached many business, political, and military challenges in the same way that he tackled the building of the greenhouse. "Personal contact, correspondence, and the printed word: All gave Washington complementary ways of learning about gardens, about greenhouses, about anything," Hayes writes.[19]

Washington's inquisitiveness and methodical research led him in the 1760s to take the bold step of abandoning tobacco, then the most common cash crop in his native Virginia. Washington stopped planting it because of taxes and duties that reduced his profits and the fact that the tobacco crop was hurting Mount Vernon's soil. According to Dennis J. Pogue, former Mount Vernon director of restoration, "By 1766 the disappointingly low prices that he was receiving in return for his tobacco harvest convinced Washington that he would be better off devoting the labor of his workers to producing other commodities that had a more dependable payoff."[20]

An inveterate experimentalist in agricultural matters, Washington grew hundreds of crops over the years at Mount Vernon, many of which were imported from Europe. (And yes, he did grow hemp, but there is no evidence that he smoked it in marijuana.) For his main cash crop, however, he chose wheat.

Washington also "farmed" the Potomac for shad, herring, and other fish. His fishery consisted of rowboats and large nets, and in a six-week fishing season each spring, Washington's men netted about 1.5 million fish. He used the inedible portions as fertilizer.[21]

Meanwhile, after retiring from the presidency, Washington built a distillery. The whiskey was made largely from crops grown at Mount Vernon, and corn, malted barley, and rye were mixed into boiling water to make a mash in 120-gallon barrels. The process is now regularly reenacted at Mount Vernon, thanks to a grant from the Distilled Spirits Council of the United States. A few times a year, Washington's whiskey is made using one of the old recipes and even sold to visitors.

Washington also played an overlooked role in assisting America's first generation of inventors. Even before he was president, all sorts of tinkerers would come to Mount Vernon to present him with their latest gadgets and seek letters of endorsement and/or his assistance in obtaining a state patent. (The U.S. Patent Office would not be created until Washington signed the Patent Act of 1790 in his second year as president.)

David Humphreys, an aide to Washington during the war, observed these inventors when he was a houseguest at Mount Vernon in the 1780s. Remarking on Washington's kindness to these visitors, Humphreys writes, "Mechanical inventions are frequently submitted for his approbation & natural curiosities presented for his investigations."[22] Humphreys marveled at the sheer number of such visitors and pieces of correspondence and wondered how they did not overwhelm their host. "Did he not husband every moment to the best advantage, it would not be in his power to notice the vast variety of objects that claim his attention."[23]

Washington also found time to tinker with "objects" of his own. He was constantly making improvements to farm equipment, such as plows. He even helped to create new breeds of plants and animals. Thus Washington brought the mule to America by crossbreeding horses and Spanish donkeys. Seeing another profit-making venture, he started a breeding service and sold mules across the nation, promoting them as an efficient alternative to horses for plowing.

This book will also show how, in his private business dealings, Washington helped lay the groundwork for innovations that changed America and the world. Thus in addition to introducing many new crops, fertilizers, tools, and machinery to American agriculture, Washington also took under his wing the American inventor James Rumsey, whose original steamboat design influenced Robert Fulton's more successful model and thereby changed the face of American transportation.

There are many things that may be "unknowable" about Washington, but his business dealings are a meticulously documented open book. Since the age of 14, Washington kept and preserved his diaries, correspondence, business ledgers, and many of his receipts. He arranged these papers in chronological order and by name and subject. And he took them nearly everywhere he went, employing special efforts to protect them. As the historian Paul Johnson notes, Washington took his archive with him to war, and his guards were under strict instructions "to protect it with their lives and hustle it to a secret place of safety."[24]

According to Johnson, the papers—sold by the Washington family to the Library of Congress in 1832—occupy 163 linear feet of shelving and 124 reels of microfilm.[25] Many of these papers are now online, but there are thousands of business-related documents that have yet to be published in any form.

It's a different story with some of Washington's more personal papers, particularly the correspondence with his wife, Martha. After George's death, Martha burned nearly all the letters they had written to each other.

But these gaps should not prevent us from attempting to know either George or Martha from the business correspondence and papers they left behind. For them, as for entrepreneurs today, their business pursuits were personal. They poured their passions, creativity, and ingenuity into growing Mount Vernon and its enterprises.

And when George saw what they had built coming under threat from increasingly oppressive British taxes and regulations, it motivated him to lead the fight both for his own liberties and those of his countrymen.

This is a story—told through the careful examination of primary documents—of an innovative entrepreneur who forged a nation through the leadership and management skills he developed in the burgeoning American business world.

CHAPTER 1

IRON ROOTS: HOW THE WASHINGTON FAMILY'S FORTUNES ROSE, FELL, AND ROSE AGAIN

Contemporary View of the Potomac River from Mount Vernon's Mansion House

Photo by Kristen H. Murray

THE WASHINGTON NAME DERIVED FROM THAT OF GEORGE Washington's paternal ancestors, the Wessyngtons. From the thirteenth century through the middle of the seventeenth, the Wessyngton/Washington family was prominent in areas of Northern England, and its members were successful as farmers, merchants, and in other jobs that carried status. George's great-great-grandfather, Lawrence Washington, was born in Northamptonshire in 1604 and became a pastor.

In Europe and later in colonial America, colleges existed primarily to prepare young men to be ministers. Lawrence studied at Oxford University's Brasenose College, receiving his degree in 1623. Ten years later, he would become the rector, or administrative leader, of the church of the affluent village of Purleigh in the county of Essex. Lawrence's son, and George's great-grandfather, John Washington was born in Purleigh in 1634.[1]

When the English Civil War broke out in the 1640s, the Washingtons were squarely on the side of the king, and the family suffered greatly because of it. When Essex was captured by Puritans fighting for Parliamentary rule, the Rev. Lawrence Washington was stripped of his clerical position and given the lowly position of vicar, an assistant cleric, at the poor parish of Little Braxted in Essex.[2]

Lawrence Washington died in poverty in 1654, and all hope for his children seemed to be dashed. But his eldest son, John, proved to be very resourceful. After serving as apprentice to a merchant who imported tobacco from the American colonies, John entered the trade himself, investing in a ship and sailing to Virginia.[3] Bad fortune seemed to follow John as a harrowing winter storm sank the ship and all its cargo in the Potomac River on its return voyage. But John took this as a sign that he should stay in Virginia for good and immediately went to work to build his fortune in the new colony.[4]

Biographer Ron Chernow notes the parallels between John Washington's ascent in America and that of his great-grandson George. "One marvels at the speed at which the young man prospered in the New World, exhibiting certain traits—a bottomless appetite for land, an avidity for public office, and a zest for frontier combat—that foreshadowed his great-grandson's rapid ascent in the world."[5] John acquired land at a rapid pace, both from wheeling and dealing for deserted lands and small forests and through the "headright" system by which a colonist received a land grant for bringing over settlers at his own expense. John would accumulate more than 10,000 acres in his lifetime and would operate a mill and a tavern. John would also serve in Virginia's colonial legislative body, the House of Burgesses.[6]

In addition, John started another Washington family tradition that would be carried on by his great-grandsons Lawrence and George: advancing socially and economically by "marrying up." The Washingtons were hard working and enterprising and they attracted wealthy women with their ambition.

John married Anne Pope, whose father, Colonel Nathaniel Pope, was a prosperous tobacco planter. They had three children, the eldest of whom, Lawrence, would become George Washington's grandfather. Lawrence didn't add that much land to his inheritance—only about 400 acres—but he too married well. Lawrence wed Mildred Warner, daughter of wealthy Gloucester County tobacco planter Augustine Warner, Jr. In 1694, Lawrence and Mildred would give Augustine's name to their second son, who would become the father of our first president.

Augustine Washington didn't inherit much, as by custom and the law of primogeniture the firstborn son most often inherited the bulk of the estate. Augustine received 1,100 acres—not an insignificant amount of land, but a fraction of his father's holdings. But he did inherit the ambition of his grandfather John Washington. And he developed some savvy about profiting from economic changes that was transmitted to his son George.

When Augustine wed Jane Butler she brought 600 acres of land under his control.[7] With this as a foundation, he began purchasing and trading land to build his estate.

Augustine was one of the first to figure out that in the coming industrial age, a land's value would be determined not just by the crops it could grow, but by the resources that could be extracted from it. The early 1700s was the dawn of the Industrial Revolution in Great Britain, and the number one material to keep that revolution going was iron, something of which Britain was in short supply.

The colonists found iron in Virginia shortly after they established the first permanent English settlement in Jamestown in 1607. The next year, colony leader Captain John Smith wrote to a friend in England that "Yron" was Jamestown's "best commoditie" and said that "little chissels" had already been made from an iron ore deposit there.[8] Virginia colonists found a few more deposits in the coming years, but it would be another century before there would be significant enough production for export. Events across the ocean—in both Great Britain and far-off destinations such as Sweden and Russia—would lead to an iron boom in Virginia that would shape the life of the man who would become the first American president.

Throughout the seventeenth century, England relied heavily on imports of raw iron from Sweden to meet its manufacturing needs, including ships for the British navy. But in the early years of the eighteenth century, Sweden's iron exports dropped dramatically due to the effects of the Great Northern War, which pitted the Swedish Empire against Russia. Sweden also hiked export duties on iron from 10 to 25 percent to raise revenue for the war. These factors caused Swedish iron exports to Great Britain to virtually cease by 1718, and they only slowly recovered after Sweden and Russia ceased hostilities in 1721.[9] Desperate for another source of iron, the British looked to spur action in colonies where ore deposits had been found.

In 1720, a group of British investors formed the Principio Company to acquire land in colonies with iron ore deposits and to build blast furnaces to smelt the ore into iron bars. The iron would then be shipped back to Great Britain to be made into finished goods. In 1722, Principio began construction of an iron mine and furnace in Cecil County, Maryland, near the border of neighboring Delaware.

Principio's agents and others looking to get rich

prospected for iron ore across the Mid-Atlantic colonies. Deposits were soon found along the Accokeek Creek in Northern Virginia, where Augustine Washington owned property.

Principio tried to buy this land on the cheap, offering Augustine cash and some of his favorite wine to sweeten the deal. But Augustine proved himself to be a brilliant negotiator and entrepreneur in his own right. He acquired all the nearby land with iron that he could. Then he agreed to build a furnace on one of his properties.

In return, Augustine asked for an ownership stake in the Principio Company, giving him one-sixth of the firm's profits and an opt-out clause to negotiate an even better contract should Principio achieve success.[10]

The ore used in furnaces in Maryland and Virginia was a coarse, dark-brown sandstone native to the region. A sledgehammer broke the ore into small pieces. Charcoal—made by colliers who burned wood in nearby forests—served as fuel, and oyster shells removed impurities as the ore was transformed into molten metal. Once a fire was started, precise quantities of charcoal, ore, and oyster shells were added to the furnace every few minutes.[11]

Although George Washington would never come into full possession of either the iron-making property or his father's share in the Principio Company, his life was shaped to a significant degree by his father's iron venture. George would make and acquire new tools made of iron material, such as plows, while the smelting facility on Augustine's land foreshadowed the "industrial village" George would create at Mount Vernon. A ban on manufacturing of iron products in the colonies imposed by Great Britain some three decades later would stoke Washington's first thoughts of armed revolt.[12]

As Augustine's fortunes increased, however, he would also suffer personal tragedy. To finalize the details of the contract with Principio, Augustine traveled to London and took along his two young sons, Lawrence and Augustine, Jr., leaving behind Jane and their four-year-old daughter, also named Jane. With a lucrative contract from Principio in hand, he enrolled his sons in the prestigious Appleby boarding school in Leicestershire, England. Upon returning to Virginia in the spring of 1730, however, he discovered that his wife had suddenly died the previous November, leaving him a widower with three children to look after.

Within a year, Augustine would marry 23-year-old Mary Ball, the strong-willed woman who would become George Washington's mother. Mary had some wealth in land and livestock, but she had also experienced her share of hard knocks.

Augustine was about 15 years older than Mary. But the difference in ages of Mary's own parents was much larger than that. Her father, Joseph Ball, a plantation owner and lieutenant colonel in the Lancaster County militia, was a 58-year-old widower and the father of adult children when he married Mary's mother, a young widow with two children of her own. Joseph died in his early sixties when Mary was three. Her mother remarried and then died when Mary was 12, after which she was shuttled around to live with different relatives. Mary survived this instability by developing a strong independent streak. Her toughness may have turned off other suitors—23 was an "old maid" age in a time when most women married in their teens—but she was probably just what Augustine needed.

Overseeing the iron furnaces and dealing with the British co-owners of Principio meant that Augustine was away much of the time, and Mary was left to run the homestead, which was its own small-business enterprise. According to Lengel, Mary's responsibilities included "overseeing and keeping accounts; directing purchase from everything from food to furniture, clothes, and home improvements and repairs; instructing slaves and workmen; and seeing to the children's needs, discipline and education." Mary and Augustine would soon have a big brood to look after. Their firstborn child would be a boy they named George.

The father of our country took his first breath on February 22, 1732, in a house that his father had built along Pope's Creek in Westmoreland County, part of Virginia's Northern Neck Peninsula that sits between the Chesapeake Bay and the Potomac and Rappahannock Rivers. George would soon be followed by his sister Betty and brothers Samuel, John, and Charles. Augustine and Mary's sixth child, Mildred, would die during infancy. In 1735 George's older half-sister Jane would also die, at age 12.

When George was two, the Washingtons moved about 70 miles north to land on the banks of the Potomac bordered by the Little Hunting and Dogue Run creeks. The land had been in George's family since his great-grandfather received it through a grant from Lord Thomas

Culpeper. Augustine purchased the property from his sister Mildred in 1726.[13]

This land would one day be christened Mount Vernon and would become the base of George Washington's many agricultural, industrial, and entrepreneurial endeavors. But he would only acquire the land through his own diligent efforts and a series of twists and turns. George Washington's career as an entrepreneur would begin some 40 miles south of Mount Vernon, on a farm that was much more modest.

CHAPTER 2

THE EDUCATION OF AN ENTREPRENEUR: AN EIGHTEENTH-CENTURY BOYHOOD

Mount Vernon Today from Across the Potomac River

Before he became one of our most consequential presidents, Woodrow Wilson was professor of jurisprudence and political economy at Princeton University. But he was also a native of Virginia and had a longtime interest in the background of the first president, who hailed from his home state. Wilson's *George Washington*, first published in 1896, was one of the first scholarly biographies of the father of our country.

In the book, Wilson notes that Washington "had a great zest for business." He attributes this "zest" to lessons Washington learned in his boyhood: "The practical genius . . . had shone in him almost prematurely as a boy."[1] If so, it is undoubtedly because circumstances conspired to make him grow up fast.

When Washington was born in 1732, the American colonies—and particularly colonial Virginia—had a rigid aristocratic class structure adapted from that of Great Britain. As Wilson points out: "Englishmen in Virginia were in no way radically distinguishable from Englishmen in England . . . Their tastes and temperament, spite of change and seclusion, they had in common with Englishmen at home."[2] Washington's family wasn't at the bottom of this structure, but they were nowhere near the top.

Meanwhile his father was always moving around to take advantage of new opportunities. After Augustine moved his family from Virginia's Northern Neck to the land further north that would become Mount Vernon, he moved the brood south again—about 40 miles—in 1738 to a home outside of Fredericksburg that would later be known as Ferry Farm.

The prime reason for this move seemed to be not the quality of the farmland but its proximity to Augustine's iron mining and furnace operations. Ferry Farm was about six miles away from the Accokeek mine, enabling Augustine to take a more active role in its operations. This—according to historian James Thomas Flexner—needed to be done. "The iron mine was showing signs of becoming exhausted: if money were to be made, Augustine must be on the scene," Flexner writes.[3]

The long-gone house that Augustine built for his growing family, though larger than the rustic cabin of the popular lore about George Washington's childhood that began with Mason Locke Weems' largely discredited *Life of Washington* (which also originated the "cherry tree" legend), was still rather modest and tightly spaced. Drawing from an inventory list Augustine had made, Flexner describes the home as "a moderate-sized wooden farm-house with four rooms on the ground floor, two above." He adds, "Crowding is indicated; comfort, but little elegance."[4] An archaeological excavation in 2008 that found the precise location of the house, a model of which is being rebuilt as of this writing, established its dimensions as $53' \times 28'$.[5]

George's status declined further when his father died in 1743. Augustine's precise cause of death remains unknown. Early biographers of George, such as Washington Irving, attributed Augustine's death to "gout in the stomach." Modern historians say pneumonia may have been the cause.[6] Whichever the case, it was not uncommon in that time for routine illnesses to result in death for children and adults. George was then 11 and his older brothers—half-brothers from his father's first marriage—received the bulk of Augustine's estate.

What George did inherit proved to be—at least at first—more of a burden than a blessing. He received ownership of Ferry Farm, half of a tract of 4,360 acres, ten slaves, and three lots in the city of Fredericksburg. These holdings were to be administered by his mother until he was of age. As Flexner writes, "George's share sounded more impressive than it was" as Ferry farm was "far from fertile" and the other land was "unimportant" and "of little value."[7]

Both the shortage of funds and the responsibilities of assisting his mother in running Ferry Farm meant that George did not get the opportunity to go to England for formal schooling in his teenage years, as his father and older brothers had. His formal schooling most likely ended before he was a teenager. But Washington's *learning*—from both books and other people—continued throughout his life.

"Washington's formal education had come to an end when he was fourteen or fifteen," writes Flexner. "Only in the mathematical bases for surveying had it carried him beyond what would today be considered the elementary school level. Everything else he came to know he taught himself from experience, conversation, or the printed page. The world was his university, and for a man of George Washington's gifts and temperament it is not a bad one."[8]

Despite this generous assessment, we now know that Washington digested a lot more of the "printed page" than Flexner and other historians had previously thought. Scholars—most notably Kevin J. Hayes in his 2017 biography *George Washington: A Life in Books*—are finding that Washington read constantly and relied on the knowledge he discovered in books for nearly every major decision he made.

Much about Washington's early education is unknown, as there are few papers that survive from that time. Among them there are reading and spelling exercises from his youth, but nothing to indicate who his teachers were or what schools he may have attended. If Washington ever sat down and wrote about his childhood, as both Jefferson and Franklin did, these writings have been lost.[9]

Since others recalled him as a schoolmate, young George probably did have at least some classroom learning with children his own age. His childhood education probably also included learning from one or more private tutors when Augustine was still alive and the family would have been in a better position to afford it.[10]

But Washington was also fortunate in having parents who were avid readers, and they evidently passed on their love of books to him. Augustine Washington's estate inventory shows that he owned some of the great works of literature, including a six-volume set of the works of William Shakespeare and Pope's translation of *The Iliad*. He had a Bible and the *Book of Common Prayer*. There was also a history of the Church of England and eight volumes of the Rev. Dr. Samuel Clarke's ten-volume *Sermons*. Clarke, who was considered an important philosopher as well as a theologian, argued that God is revealed through observing nature and scientific laws.[11] He was one of many authors in the eighteenth century who urged his readers to make use of any material object to reflect on the wonder of God.

George's mother owned many books as well. Mary's relationship with George was strained, and she could be very demanding. In the 1780s, she petitioned the Virginia government for relief even though George had purchased a stately home for her in Fredericksburg and took care of many of her expenses.[12] However, Mary still had some undoubtedly positive influences on her son's success as both an entrepreneur and statesmen.

Some historians have downplayed Mary's intellectual capacities. For example, in *Washington: A Life*, biographer Ron Chernow asserts that Mary Washington was barely literate. He calls her an "unlettered countrywoman" and claims that she "betrayed little interest in the larger world." Yet he notes just a few pages later that Mary read to her children daily portions of the book *Contemplations: Moral and Divine* by Sir Matthew Hale.[13] Chernow leaves readers with the impression that this book was on the same level as nursery rhymes. But *Contemplations* is by no means an easy read. Hale was a distinguished judge, lawyer, and member of Parliament, and his writings delved into law and science as well as religion. *Contemplations* is 558 pages long and tries to explain the precepts of Christianity in light of the advances in knowledge of the Enlightenment age.

In his recent book, historian Hayes cites Mary's grandson and George Washington's nephew as recalling that his grandmother would read Bible verses aloud to the family every Sunday night and would dramatically represent both the saints and angels.[14] He also notes that Mary owned many other lengthy, serious books.[15]

Mary's library reflects a particular interest in prayer and meditation. Among her books were John Scott's *The Christian Life* and the Rev. James Hervey's two-volume *Meditations and Contemplations*. Like the book by Clarke that was owned by George's father, Hervey and Scott recommended finding God through contemplating the laws of nature and the properties of certain natural objects. They also stressed meditation as a way to get closer to God, not in the Eastern sense of "egoless" contemplation but in the sense of deep intellectual reflection on first causes.[16]

Mary appears to have passed on the practice of meditation to her son George. As Hayes notes:

> When faced with conflict during wartime . . . or contradictory views during his presidency, Washington applied his meditative powers to devise solutions to the difficulties he faced. After a battle had been won or controversy resolved, he meditated further to help understand the meaning of his accomplishments . . . For George Washington, personal experiences became texts to be used for meditation, a process and practice that shaped his decisions on the battlefield and in the political arena.[17]

Washington would also apply the knowledge of mathematics he learned as a boy to garner successes and victories on the battlefield and in the colonial business world.

In addition to learning the basics of arithmetic, geometry, and other branches of math in the classroom or from his tutors, Washington had some fun books that combined math with adventure. One of the books young George probably read was William Mather's *The Young Man's Companion*, subtitled *Arithmetick Made Easy*.[18] As described by Hayes, the book "presents an eclectic mix of useful information, explaining how to write English, create basic legal forms, understand world geography, maintain a garden, manage fruit trees, and prepare useful medicine."[19]

Mather's book also contained a tip that Washington may have used to help win the war against the British. The book gave young boys a simple recipe for invisible ink, which involved mixing ink with a few drops of brandy.[20]

As those who have read Brian Kilmeade and Don Yaeger's *George Washington's Secret Six*, or watched the AMC series *Turn*, are aware, Washington and his Culper Ring spy network used invisible ink to send messages to one another. Washington worked with physician James Jay (brother of future Supreme Court justice John Jay) to develop a state-of-the-art ink that could be made visible only with the use of another chemical.[21] But he may well have first learned about it from Mather.

Washington also learned math as a boy from John Seller's *Practical Navigation*. The book also taught lessons in geography, astronomy, and, most importantly, the relatively new field of cartography.[22]

Throughout his life, Washington was an avid map-reader and mapmaker. He drew or annotated at least 110 maps of areas he was surveying, including battlefields and the grounds of his own residence.[23] Washington also collected at least 190 maps that he kept in his Mount Vernon library.[24]

Washington's love of cartography—then still in its infancy—would serve him well on the battlefield. In a detailed letter in 1777 in which Washington pressed the Continental Congress for provisions, including more beer and rum for the troops ("Beer or Cyder seldom comes within the verge of the Camp, and Rum in much too small quantities"), he requested that it also foot the bill for services from Robert Erskine, North America's top mapmaker at that time. "A good Geographer to Survey the roads and take sketches of the Country where the Army is to Act would be extremely useful and might be attended with exceeding valuable consequences," Washington explained.[25]

By May 1780, Erskine and his staff had drawn more than 250 maps.[26] Erskine's maps of the Hudson Highlands region of New York were particularly valuable in helping Washington prevent the British from taking control of the Hudson River Valley, thereby dividing New England from the Middle and Southern colonies.[27]

His love of maps would also serve Washington well in his various entrepreneurial ventures. In fact, he made heavy use of maps—and drew plenty of his own—in his first job as a surveyor of the Virginia frontier.

After Augustine died and left no provisions for George's education, the boy knew that his options were limited. Like many young colonials he yearned to see the wider world and originally sought a career in the Royal Navy, following in the footsteps of his older brother

Lawrence, who had served in a Virginia naval regiment under the command of Vice Admiral Edward Vernon (later to become the namesake of Washington's estate). But George's mother contravened these plans after her brother Joseph, who had previously moved to England, raised a series of strong objections.

Joseph Ball's letter, which has fortunately been preserved, explained that a career in the Royal Navy wasn't quite the golden opportunity it appeared to be. Superior officers would work George "like a dog" and opportunities for advancement would be limited. Even if George should eventually become the captain of a ship, an ordinary farmer "may live more comfortably and leave his family in better bread than such a master of the ship can," Ball wrote. He concluded with this practical advice for his nephew: "He must not be hasty to be rich but must go on gently and with patience as things will naturally go."[28]

Mary Washington has been criticized by many of her son's biographers as holding him back from the navy for selfish reasons—and it may be true that she preferred to keep him close to home where he could care for her and look after her interests. Yet in her recent sympathetic biography, *The Widow Washington*, Martha Saxton argues that Mary simply had the natural concern of many parents when it comes to sending their children off to war and other dangerous pursuits. Saxton writes, "It is hard to dispute her good sense in keeping her fourteen-year-old son out of the British Navy, a singularly dangerous institution in the eighteenth century."[29]

Whatever Mary's reasons, her decision was a fortunate one for the new nation, for if George had joined the navy as he wished, he might never have come back to lead our forces in the Revolutionary War.

✱ ✱ ✱

George had loved visiting the Mount Vernon estate since he was a boy, but it was never meant to be his. The land had been in Washington's family since 1674, and Augustine had bought it from his sister Mildred in 1726. But when Augustine died in 1743, the estate went to George's half-brother Lawrence, Augustine's son from his previous marriage.

Fourteen years older than George, Lawrence served as a surrogate father and mentor for his younger half-sibling, and George began spending much time at Mount Vernon. Sitting on the banks of the Potomac River and then functioning primarily as a tobacco plantation, Mount Vernon was considerably more upscale than the simple Ferry Farm where Washington lived with his mother and younger siblings. As Willard Sterne Randall puts it, "Nothing at Ferry Farm had prepared George for a house where everyone wore shoes and where there were separate parlors so that one group could dance or play music while another played whist and loo."[30]

Then there was Belvoir, the even grander brick mansion four miles downstream that was home to the Fairfax family, one of the most prominent families in Virginia. Through Lawrence's recent marriage to Anne Fairfax, George became part of the extended family and he frequently visited Belvoir, where Anne's relatives took him under their wing. Anne's father, William Fairfax, introduced George to the elite sport of fox hunting and gave

him access to his vast library, with its many books on subjects from science and philosophy to history and agriculture.[31] He also took George on inspections of Belvoir's
farms, mills, and other business operations.

These "real world" lessons coincided with George's
other studies, which included making meticulous copies
of business forms. As Woodrow Wilson notes, Washington's exercise books were filled with "careful copies of
legal and mercantile papers, bills of exchange, bills of
sale, bonds, indentures, land warrants, leases, deeds, and
wills, as if he meant to be a lawyer or merchant's clerk." As
Lawrence and the Fairfaxes traded extensively with English merchants, they "looked upon such forms of business paper as quite as useful as ploughs and hogsheads."

Another family member who took an interest in
young George was William's cousin, Lord Thomas Fairfax. Born in Leeds Castle in Kent and educated at Oxford, Lord Thomas arrived in the colonies and settled
at Belvoir in 1747 to oversee the vast swath of lands he
owned in the Northern Neck of Virginia. He had hired
William, who had lived in the colonies for more than two
decades, as his agent.

Like his cousin, Thomas Fairfax was a voracious
reader. A portrait shows him holding a book, with his
right thumb saving his place in the volume.[32] Among the
vast assets he brought to America was his extensive collection of books and literary magazines. Lord Fairfax introduced George to *The Spectator*, and Washington wrote in
his journal how much he enjoyed it.[33]

As well, George's youthful friendship with William's
son, George William Fairfax, and his wife, Sally, would

last for the rest of their lives. The young aristocrats taught George much about clothing, manners, and social customs at balls and other high society events.[34]

But the Fairfax men also taught George a thing or two about roughing it, and in doing so they helped lay the foundation for his life as an entrepreneur and, indirectly, as a military leader and statesman.

CHAPTER 3

A DIRTY JOB: THE ORIGINS OF WASHINGTON'S CAREER AS A SURVEYOR AND LAND SPECULATOR

Washington's Weather Vane
atop the Mansion House

Photo by Kristen H. Murray

As a middle child, Washington didn't inherit nearly as much as his older half-brothers. But he did inherit some old equipment his father had used to survey land. This gear included a pole and chain link to measure distances as well as a compass on top of a tripod. Surveyors placed the tripod firmly in the ground so the attached compass could measure angles between two points.[1] Washington used this equipment to launch a lucrative career that would set him on the path to greater success.

First jobs are often important to great entrepreneurs, even if they ultimately make their fortunes in a different field. From his first job fixing pocket watches when he was 13, Henry Ford got the idea of mass producing them so they would be more affordable for average people. Ford never became a watchmaker, but he refined the idea of mass production and later applied it to cars. In a similar way, George Washington used his first job as a surveyor to learn important skills and make connections that would serve him for the rest of his life.

Washington first took up surveying when he was around 14. After he ran surveying lines in the fields of Ferry Farm, he conducted a survey of a turnip field at his brother's estate, which would eventually become Mount Vernon. Lawrence took note of George's interest in the craft and would soon provide him with an opportunity to establish himself as a professional surveyor.

The Fairfaxes had acquired five million acres in Virginia between the Potomac and Rappahannock Rivers. This vast swath of land, which now encompasses much of the Northern Virginia suburbs of Washington, DC, was then largely undeveloped. Not only was there a lack of knowledge about the conditions and resources of the area, it wasn't even known which parts were populated, as squatters were illegally taking up residence there and American Indian tribes had long inhabited some sections. In 1748, therefore, the Fairfaxes put together a surveying team to explore the land and formally establish its boundaries. George's intelligence, good manners, and burgeoning surveying skills had won the confidence of the elder Fairfaxes, and they hired George to assist in the important job of surveying their vast holdings.

Surveying undeveloped land that was then considered part of the frontier was a dirty job even for Washington's time. As he made his way through the mud and muck in the areas near the Blue Ridge Mountains, Washington paid close attention to the two leaders of the expedition: experienced surveyor James Genn and 24-year-old George William Fairfax, who was representing the family. But there were some things he had to learn on his own.

In Washington's journal of this expedition, his earliest known piece of extended writing, he vividly describes his first encounter with backwoods lodging. After a long day of surveying land that was largely wilderness, the trio stayed overnight at a shack owned by some settlers. After the supper provided by the hosts, the party was ushered into a small chamber where they were to sleep. Washington was tired and made the mistake of taking a bed, wondering why Fairfax and Genn had chosen to sleep on the floor. He soon found out.

From Washington's journal: "I, not being as good a

woodsman as the rest of my company, stripped myself very orderly and went into the bed, as they called it, when to my surprise, I found it to be nothing but a little straw matted together, without sheets or anything else, but only one threadbare blanket, with double its weight of vermin, such as lice, fleas, etc."[2]

Washington carefully arose from the bed. "I put on my clothes, and lay as my companions [on the floor]," he wrote in the journal.[3]

As for the rest of the trip, George and his companions roughed it in the great outdoors. As Washington recalled, "Our spits were forked sticks, our plate was a large chip, as for dishes we had none."[4]

Despite these privations, Washington worked diligently at measuring and observing the land. As described by Willard Sterne Randall, Washington was tasked to "manhandle the supplies, care for the horses, clear the underbrush, haul the [measuring] chains, and hold steady the rod for the sightings."[5]

But the budding entrepreneur still found time to marvel at the untamed landscape—and to consider how it might be profitable. In the majestic Shenandoah Valley, Washington admired the "most beautiful groves of sugar trees" and developed his nascent skill at studying land and determining the best uses for it—a skill he would later utilize as a land speculator and innovative entrepreneurial farmer, as well as for gaining the edge on a battlefield.

When the four-week expedition was finished, Washington had proven his mettle to Genn and the Fairfaxes, and with their support he began to get other jobs assisting Virginia's top surveyors. In addition to learning from his various employers, Washington read constantly about the latest trends in the profession. From the Fairfax family library, Washington borrowed William Leybourn's *The Compleat Surveyor*, one of the first surveying texts to incorporate modern geometry into the surveyor's measurements. Washington also acquired Guillaume Francois Antoine L'Hospital's *Analytik Treatise of Conick Sections*, which delved into the shapes formed from sections of a cone, such as circles and ellipses, and showed their practical application in surveying. This was cutting edge for the eighteenth century, "beyond the reach of most contemporary students," according to Hayes.[6]

Soon, as other landowners heard about Washington's knowledge, skill, and sheer tenacity, he launched a lucrative freelance career.

In 1749, he assisted in surveying the contours for a new town at the head of the Potomac River, a few miles from Mount Vernon. Today, Alexandria, Virginia, is a prominent suburb of Washington, DC. Many of the streets in downtown Alexandria still run in the design that Washington helped to create. According to William Seale, historian and former curator of cultural history at the Smithsonian Institution: "They platted the streets on a grid, as regular as graf paper, with the greatest thrift of space. One public space and only one was permitted—the Market Square—and it was for the conduct of business . . . Even the town pumps stood at intersections, so as not to waste land that might bring in money."[7]

Washington soon became one of the most sought-after surveyors in Virginia. In 1749, just after finishing the survey of Alexandria, the 17-year-old Washington was chosen to be official surveyor of Culpeper County, which is at the foot of the Blue Ridge Mountains near the Rappahannock River. But because the county was already largely settled, Washington still had the opportunity to conduct freelance surveys.

Over the next three years, Washington conducted almost 200 surveys, mostly for private clients outside Culpeper County. As Edward Lengel writes, his "solid work guaranteed a litigation-free landowning experience for his many customers, and word got around."[8]

Still in his late teens, Washington was suddenly earning more from surveying over a few months than many Virginia farmers and merchants made in a year. According to British historian Stephen Brumwell, Washington earned an estimated 400 British pounds in three years working as a surveyor. By contrast, the best the average craftsman could hope for was an annual wage of 35 pounds.[9] As Ron Chernow observes, "For a young man who could not afford corn for his horse a year earlier, it was a startling and nearly dreamlike elevation in status."[10]

Washington took a disciplined approach to how he budgeted his earnings. Flexner writes that beginning in 1747, "Washington was keeping careful accounts of his cash expenditures, down to his last half-penny, a habit he was to continue long after he had left financial stringency behind him."[11]

He did buy some fine new clothes and gambled in the occasional card game. But mostly he used the proceeds to buy new surveying equipment and began investing in some of the undeveloped land he was surveying, using the inside track that surveyors had to obtain prime tracts of real estate. In 1750, Washington paid 112 pounds to James McCracken for 456 acres in the Shenandoah Valley. Two years later, he bought 552 acres nearby from Captain George Johnston for 115 pounds. He would also frequently acquire some acres of land as payment for surveying. From 1750 to 1753, Washington acquired 2,315 acres of fertile land in the Shenandoah Valley.[12]

Washington would lease much of this land to tenant farmers, a practice he would continue for the rest of his life. Sociologist Wilma Dunaway writes that "independent tenant farming emerged historically on the Appalachian frontier as a technique by which absentee investors cleared trees, opened new roads, and improved land for resale."[13] Washington would often take a portion of the tenant's crops as payment, and his leases would specify which type of crops the tenants could grow.

Washington's disciplined approach to money also led to his becoming somewhat of a community lender. Flexner writes that "as is often the case with those who watch their money, he usually had cash in his pocket," and that meant that "he was continually making small loans to richer friends and relatives."[14] It may seem odd that richer people would seek to borrow money from Washington. The reasons for that were twofold. First, then as now, people who have a lot of nice things are often overextended and may need cash to pay off a debt that's coming due. Second, currency was always short in the colonies as Britain didn't have national banks or mints to directly issue its currency outside the mother country. So colonists would use barter, foreign currency such as Spanish dollars, and IOUs such as tobacco warehouse receipts in lieu of British pounds. When Washington completed his surveying jobs, he would always get paid in the popular currencies of which other colonists were frequently short, even if they had extensive landholdings.

Washington learned many lessons about hard work, thrift, and perseverance in this period. Like many other entrepreneurs, he also learned that government rules and regulations can have unintended consequences. Some three decades later, British taxes, regulations, and trade barriers would ultimately lead Washington and other colonists to revolution. But as a teenage entrepreneur trying to get his surveying business off the ground, Washington dealt with his first strands of red tape from the colonial government of Virginia.

First, there were its price controls on land surveys. The Virginia legislature set a rate that surveyors legally couldn't exceed. But Washington wanted more, and his customers were willing to pay it. So he appears to have openly defied the price control laws, often charging twice the mandated maximum price set by the Virginia government.[15]

There do not appear to have been any government officials who confronted Washington over his flouting of price controls. But another government mandate would not be so easy to get around. This one had to do with occupational licensing laws, which limit opportunities and frustrate entrepreneurial startups to this day.[16]

In eighteenth-century Virginia, county surveyors were licensed by the College of William and Mary in Williamsburg, which was then Virginia's capital. When the college was chartered by the Virginia government in 1693, it was given the power to appoint all surveyors in the colony. The legislature also gave the college the right to collect one-sixth of those surveyors' fees, from both their public and private surveying jobs.

When the college appointed Washington as surveyor of Culpeper County in 1749, it allowed relatively free entry into surveying and didn't exercise its taxing power fully. But a few years later, in the early 1750s, it started exercising its prerogative to take the full amount.

Washington lived before the development of modern economics. But he had enough business sense to know that when taxation of a given activity becomes unduly onerous, it is time to change professions. According to Lengel, the increase in levies was a significant factor in Washington's decision to quit surveying in 1752.[17]

Other events in Washington's life factored into his decision to close his freelance surveying business. As mentioned earlier, in 1751 George dropped everything to travel to Barbados with his older brother Lawrence in hopes that the warmer climate would allow his brother to recover from what was likely tuberculosis. The trip of about four months (including approximately one month of sailing each way) was ultimately unsuccessful, as Lawrence passed away in July 1752. At this point, George began to manage Mount Vernon, first leasing it from his sister-in-law, then eventually owning it after the tragic deaths of Anne and her young daughter.

Before that, however, Washington decided to enlist in the Virginia regiment of the British military. He would get a plum appointment as major, as he had the skills and experience needed to find out where the French were settling on land claimed by Britain, a dispute that would form the basis for the French and Indian War. As Chernow explains, Washington "knew the Western Country from surveying."[18]

Indeed, Washington would find the knowledge he gained as a surveyor in his youth to be beneficial throughout his life. As Randall writes, it gave him "a basic understanding of principles that would make him a master of selecting land for cultivation and, later, for fortifications and battlefields." And as Chernow notes, "Even when he toured the 13 states as first president, he methodically reported the topographic features of places, as if he remained a working surveyor. Whether as planter or president, his study was liberally supplied with maps and charts."[19]

In fact, Washington would conduct private surveys of Mount Vernon several times throughout his life, the last one being made five weeks before he died in 1799.

CHAPTER 4

WASHINGTON'S SOCIAL NETWORK: THE KEY TO SUCCESS IN BUSINESS, LIFE, AND POLITICS

The Clerk's Office as Reconstructed at Mount Vernon

Photo by Kristen H. Murray

IT WAS THE AUTUMN OF 1783, AND GENERAL WASHINGton had time on his hands. British general Charles Cornwallis had surrendered more than two years earlier after suffering a decisive defeat at the Battle of Yorktown at the combined hands of American and French forces. Except for a few skirmishes, attacks by the British had largely ceased.

Yet there were still issues that needed to be ironed out, such as agreed-upon boundaries between the United States and the British territory that is now Canada. Meanwhile, the change in control of Parliament from the Tories to the Whigs in 1782 delayed matters even further. So until a formal treaty was signed, the Continental Army had to stand guard.

As negotiations progressed in Paris, Washington moved his headquarters to New York to keep an eye on the thousands of British troops still present there. In August of that year he moved to Rocky Hill, New Jersey, near where the Continental Congress was convening in Princeton. Martha Washington and several soldiers accompanied George to the estate rented to them by Margaret Berrien. There they would live until November, when America's delegates returned with the successfully signed treaty.

During their stay, Washington invited Thomas Paine, author of the revolutionary pamphlet *Common Sense*, to be their guest. During this visit, Washington and Paine, who also wrote about trends in science and would become a minor inventor, decided to conduct what is now considered the first major scientific experiment in the new nation.

Washington had heard stories from local residents of small fires igniting on the nearby Millstone River. Needless to say, there was disagreement and uncertainty as to their cause. Washington's interest was probably also piqued because he had become aware of fires on another river almost a decade earlier, when he was scouting real estate in what is now West Virginia. In return for his service in the French and Indian War, Great Britain had allotted Washington warrants to claim 5,000 acres along the Kanawha River, near what is now Charleston, West Virginia. After studying surveys of the land, Washington chose 250 acres along what he described in a 1775 letter as a "burning spring."[1] When bequeathing this land in his will, Washington described it as containing "so inflammable a nature as to burn as freely as spirits, and is nearly as difficult to extinguish."[2]

Washington and Paine decided to get to the bottom of this peculiar phenomenon. On the night of November 5, 1783, Washington, Paine, and some officers sailed into the river in a flat-bottomed scow. They then stirred up mud with poles, and Washington and Paine lit paper torches that they held above the water. Soon, bubbles surfaced and flames quickly covered the river's surface.

As Paine would describe it over 20 years later: "When the mud at the bottom was disturbed by the poles, the air bubbles rose fast, and I saw the fire take from General Washington's light and descend from thence to the surface of the water, in a similar manner as when a lighted candle is held so as to touch the smoke of a candle just blown out, the smoke will take fire, and the fire will descend and light up the candle. This was demonstrative evidence that what was called setting the river on fire was setting on fire the inflammable air that arose out of the mud."[3]

Washington and Paine had proven there was gas in the ground, a fact that would have major implications for energy exploration in that region, which includes the oil- and gas-rich parts of Pennsylvania. Land near Washington's "burning spring" also proved energy-rich, as some of the first oil and natural gas development in the nation occurred there in the mid-nineteenth century.[4] Scientists conducting a 2008 reenactment of the Washington-Paine experiment on the Millstone River found that the "inflammable air" igniting the river was most likely methane.[5] Professor Douglas Eveleigh of Rutgers University, who organized the reenactment, writes that the Washington-Paine experiment along with a similar experiment in Italy conducted in 1776 "initiated understanding of the microbial process today termed methanogenesis."[6]

The experiment shows that Washington had the same kind of scientific curiosity often associated with founding fathers such as Franklin and Thomas Jefferson. Yet Jefferson and Franklin performed many of their experiments and endeavors alone, while Washington would often find talented people and bring out their potential in joint ventures. In short, Washington was the consummate social animal, with a wide network of friends and acquaintances with whom he kept in touch and frequently collaborated.

From a young age, Washington learned to treat people from all walks of life with dignity and respect. In fact, he made a positive practice of it, as shown by his lifelong adherence to the precepts set down in a collection of 110 maxims known as *The Rules of Civility and Decent Behaviour in Company and Conversation.*

The origins of these maxims are unclear. Some of them are similar to a list of social rules from French Jesuits in the 1590s that were translated into English around 1640. Yet there are many maxims of unknown origin in Washington's collection. Some of these may have come from Washington's instructor, who is also unknown to history, or from the teenage Washington himself, based on lessons he had already learned from dealing with all kinds of people in various settings. Whichever the case, it is clear that Washington saw them as an important aid to advancing his social and economic ambitions. He copied them out by hand by the age of 16 and adhered to them religiously for the rest of his life.

The first rule is, "Every Action done in Company, ought to be with Some Sign of Respect, to those that are Present." The third is, "Shew Nothing to your Freind that may affright him."[7]

Among other things, these rules are likely to have promoted good listening skills, which Washington undoubtedly possessed. His ability to take counsel from a wide range of sources served him well in both business and war—and at the Constitutional Convention, where he famously sat listening for days and weeks on end while saying almost nothing during the official proceedings. It may also have led him to set an important political precedent by creating the president's Cabinet. Nothing in the Constitution or federal law mandates that the president convene his top officials to discuss policy issues. But Washington regularly held meetings with Treasury Secretary Alexander Hamilton, Secretary of State Thomas Jefferson, Attorney General Edmund Randolph, and Secretary of War Henry Knox. Every subsequent presidency has followed his example.

But he didn't just hear the voices of the elites. All his life, he strived to meet and learn from people from all walks of life. Part of his reason for doing this was the simple necessity of military life. As Lengel writes, "Military service is a social equalizer." As a young officer in his twenties, Washington found himself commanding troops from modest to poor backgrounds in the French and Indian War. Lengel notes that from listening to those who served under him, Washington "learned about the hardships that a day's lost pay or going without a meal—hardly gentlemen's concerns—could impose on common folk. He was not without empathy, and became their advocate."[8]

The future president would also get to know a wide variety of men through his lifelong involvement with the Freemasons, which began when the 20-year-old Washington joined a Masonic lodge in Fredericksburg, Virginia, in 1752.[9]

The Masons are a sort of paradox. Like many clubs with elaborate rituals, they have oaths of silence about what goes on at meetings. This secretiveness can on the surface seem elitist, and politicians, business tycoons, and other powerful men have always been found in their ranks. Indeed, the number of prominent men in Masonic lodges is part of what has given rise to various conspiracy theories about them.

Yet even before Washington's time, the Masons were relatively inclusive. Generally, as long as men adhered to the rules, their backgrounds didn't matter all that much. The 1723 Masonic constitution of the Grand Lodge of England, then known as the Mother Lodge of the World, declared that Freemasons should not discriminate based on religion, nationality, or even—especially amazing for the time—race. British poet and novelist Rudyard Kipling recalled joining a Masonic lodge as a young man in India in the 1880s and meeting many Muslims, Hindus, and Sikhs who were fellow members.[10]

Adherence to these principles varied from lodge to lodge, but most American lodges followed these general principles of tolerance. American Jews began joining Masonic lodges in the mid-eighteenth century, and at least one Freemason who was Jewish made a direct connection with Washington. Moses Seixas was a first-generation American whose parents had migrated from Lisbon to Newport, Rhode Island, shortly before he was born in 1744. Taking advantage of the opportunities America offered to civic-minded entrepreneurs, Seixas would become co-founder of the Bank of Rhode Island, warden of Newport's Touro Synagogue, and Grand Master of the Grand Lodge of Free and Accepted Masons of Rhode Island.

In 1790, just over a year after Washington's inauguration as president, Seixas wrote him two letters—one on behalf of the synagogue and the other on behalf of the lodge. Washington answered both letters promptly. His letter to the synagogue assured the congregants that Jews would have not just religious freedom in the new country but equal political rights as well.

Washington presented his letter of reply on the same day that he visited the synagogue during a trip to Rhode Island in August 1790. "The Children of the Stock of Abraham . . . shall sit in safety under his own vine and fig tree," Washington proclaimed. Both his letter and his visit to the synagogue have been widely praised as heralding a new chapter in history, in which religious minorities would have full citizenship of the countries in which they lived.

The letter to Seixas' Masonic lodge, by contrast, was a mere four sentences and the sentiments expressed were pretty general. Freemasons "must be promotive of private virtue and public prosperity," wrote Washington. There was, however, some significance in the way he referred to himself as a "deserving brother" of the lodge led by Seixas.[11]

Understanding people from all walks of life is also one of the keys to successful entrepreneurship. To create a market for a good or service, an aspiring entrepreneur has to be familiar with the wants and needs of those he wants as customers. Washington went into a number of businesses, from flour to distilling to blacksmithing, based on his sense of what potential customers would want. He gathered this knowledge informally from interactions with people of all kinds. He especially queried friends and employees who had visited or emigrated from other countries to get ideas for new ventures and to learn from what had worked overseas.

From the Marquis de Lafayette, the aristocratic Frenchman who volunteered his services to the Continental Army, a civilian Washington asked for French hunting hounds to breed with his foxhounds and French donkeys to breed with his horses to create mules. Lafayette provided what he asked for.[12]

Similarly, Washington was presented with the idea of building a distillery at Mount Vernon by his farm manager, James Anderson, who had emigrated to the United States from Scotland. Washington in turn sought the advice of his friend John Fitzgerald, an Irish émigré who had served as one of his top aides during the war and then became a successful merchant in Alexandria. Fitzgerald replied that a distillery was a very profitable opportunity, and Washington took his friend's advice and went ahead.[13]

Washington also maintained a large and diverse correspondence through which he forged important friendships and alliances that led to greater success, both for himself and the new nation.

Compared to Jefferson, Franklin, and Hamilton, Washington is not thought of as a particularly talented writer. But his letters and other papers are not without their virtues.

Jefferson himself praised his talents some 15 years after his death, saying that Washington "wrote readily, rather diffusely, in an easy & correct style."[14] Henrietta Liston, whose husband Robert served as minister to the United States from Great Britain during Washington's presidency, also praised Washington's style, and replied to those who suggested that a secretary wrote his letters for him: "Ill natured people said that Washington did not write his own publick letters, answers to addresses, &c. this is not true. I have known him to write in his usual impressive manner when no person was near to aid him; & what may seem conclusive,—he has always written better than the Gentleman to who the merit of his letters was ascribed."[15]

Liston wrote of Washington's "dignified manners" and remarked that he had "correct knowledge of even the etiquette of a [royal] court." How he acquired this knowledge, she pondered, "heaven knows." Both she and Jefferson were largely unaware of Washington's tremendous self-education efforts, as were most people at the time and in the generations that followed. As historian Richard Brookhiser observes, "Mrs. Liston did not know that Washington had been practicing his manners for half a century, as well as the morals that they implied."[16]

Then as now, writing timely and appreciative letters was considered part of having good manners. A teenage Washington wrote to a friend that the personal letter was "the greatest mark of friendship and esteem."[17] Just as important to Washington's early education as *The Rules of Civility* was *The Royal English Grammar* by James Greenwood, headmaster of St. Paul's School in London. As Hayes notes: "Whereas *The Rules* stressed the importance of speaking properly, Greenwood extended that idea to the realm of the written word to emphasize the social value of writing properly. In essence, Greenwood made English composition a matter of proper social conduct." The book contained numerous grammatical exercises and samples of good literary style. Washington's surviving copy of the book "reveals its use: the corners of the page are heavily worn from frequent bethumbings."[18]

Washington wrote thousands of letters during his lifetime, some of which have been published in multivolume sets, with more still waiting to be archived. He wrote for many reasons. One of his most frequent tasks was to write simple thank-you notes, a task that became more onerous as Washington became more famous. Biographer Humphreys reported that in the mid-1780s—after Washington retired as general and returned to Mount Vernon but before he became the nation's first president—"correspondencies unavoidably engross a great portion of his time." Some of this correspondence was from important domestic and foreign leaders, but much of it was what we would today call celebrity "fan mail." According to Humphreys, Washington received numerous letters "on subjects foreign to his situation, frivolous in their nature and intended merely to gratify the vanity of the writers by drawing answers from him."[19]

Keeping up with this correspondence, Humphreys wrote, was "truly distressing and almost incredible."[20] In addition to managing the enterprises at Mount Vernon—which was more than a full-time job—Washington spent hours every day reading and answering letters.[21] Finally, he hired Tobias Lear, a highly efficient private secretary who would continue serving him through his presidency.

In addition, of course, there were the correspondences that Washington himself initiated, seeking answers to questions about his business operations, military strategy, the leadership of a new country, or random things he wanted to know about the world. Just as he wrote to Margaret Carroll for advice about building and maintaining a greenhouse, Washington kept up to date on the latest farming machinery and techniques by writing to the leading agriculturalists of the day both in the United States and abroad. In particular, he kept up an extensive correspondence with famed British agriculture writer Arthur Young in the 1780s and '90s. They shared recommendations on seeds, livestock, and farm tools. Young also asked Washington about agriculture production in the United States. Young would send Washington a copy of his annual periodical *Annals of Agriculture* every year from 1784 to 1798.[22]

If Washington liked a book or pamphlet, he would frequently write to the author, both to praise him or her (Washington corresponded with at least two pioneering female authors: the historian Mercy Otis Warren and the poet Phillis Wheatley, an African American who had been freed from slavery) and to ask further questions. Washington began this habit as a young adult and continued it throughout his life. After he read George Mason's writings on how British taxation and control of the colonies' trading routes violated natural rights, Washington sought him out to discuss natural rights theory as well as ways in which the colonists could fight for these rights, such as boycotts of British goods.

Luckily, Washington didn't have to travel far to talk to Mason, whose estate was in Fairfax County, close to Mount Vernon. For those who lived further away, Washington would often make arrangements to host them and also boost their work.

The celebrated author Thomas Paine, whom Washington hosted in New Jersey in 1783, affords an interesting example. Despite making a consistent and compelling case for the colonies to break away from Great Britain,

Paine had only moved to America from England less than two years before the Declaration of Independence, settling in Philadelphia in late 1774. After Paine joined a volunteer militia in Pennsylvania, Washington gave him a prestigious post as aide-de-camp to General Nathanael Greene. In this capacity, Paine went on to publish a series of pamphlets chronicling the battles he saw.

Washington kept track of Paine and promoted his work. He ordered copies of Paine's pamphlet *The American Crisis* for the troops, and soldiers carried it with them into battle. The only known first edition of *The American Crisis* sits today in the American Philosophical Society museum in Philadelphia, stained with the blood of a soldier injured or killed while carrying it into battle.[23]

Paine and Washington would have a falling out in the 1790s over the French Revolution, after Paine attacked Washington (then president) in a scathing letter. Paine, who was then a resident of France, denounced him both for remaining neutral and not supporting the French rebels, and then for what he saw as a delay in diplomatic assistance when the rebels turned against Paine and arrested him. (James Monroe, then Washington's minister to France, would eventually secure Paine's release.)[24] However, after Washington's death, Paine recalled with fondness his friendship with Washington and their methane gas experiment.[25]

In his own time and for many years thereafter, Washington was considered an intellectual lightweight with limited interests, at least in contrast to his more brilliant associates like Hamilton, Jefferson, Adams, and Madison. In reality, Washington was a highly cultivated person who not only read widely in the scientific literature of his day but also read many fine works of literature and was particularly fond of the theater. His letters provide evidence of this. For one thing, they contain many quotes from Shakespeare, whose plays Washington had both read and seen performed.

Washington established himself as a friend to the arts and sciences even as a private citizen. After he "retired" to Mount Vernon after the war, he received dozens of visits from authors and artists, who also contributed to his heavy correspondence. Observing the bustling activity as a houseguest at Mount Vernon, Humphreys wrote, "There are many introductions sent to him annually by their authors in Europe, and there is scarcely one work written on any art, science or subject which does not seek his protection, or which is not offered to him as a token of gratitude."[26]

In fact, authors would frequently send Washington a book in order to get one of his treasured thank-you notes. As Hayes notes, "By presenting a book to General Washington, an author could receive in exchange a handwritten thank-you note from the most famous man in America."[27] These authors knew that Washington's endorsement would be of great value in further promoting their work.

However, though unfailingly gracious, Washington didn't always respond the way the authors hoped. When Jeremy Belknap, a Congregational minister in Dover, New Hampshire, sent him the first volume of his *History of New Hampshire* along with a flattering cover letter, Washington replied: "For both, I pray you accept my thanks—but my acknowledgements are more particularly due, for my favorable expression in the former, of my past efforts to support the Cause of liberty."[28]

Belknap was a bit disappointed, as it sounded like Washington liked the cover letter better than the 300-page book it had taken him more than a decade to write. Still, Washington did praise Belknap's writing of at least one document, and Belknap told his publisher that he would keep Washington's letter and "rank it among my valuables."[29] The letter ended up being more than a keepsake. As Hayes notes, "Belknap sometimes had difficulty motivating himself to write, but Washington's thank-you letter encouraged him to continue his literary efforts."[30]

When artists visited Mount Vernon, Washington frequently had to expend even more efforts, as they often wanted him to pose for hours for a painting or sculpture. Washington was reluctant at first, but his patience grew as he realized the importance of visual images.[31] After all, in the days before any type of camera existed, paintings and engravings were the only way to make the public familiar with one's face. In the 1820s and '30s, Andrew Jackson would actually invite portraitist Ralph E. W. Earl to live at the White House so that he could churn out images of the president with greater frequency.[32]

Posing was rarely easy for someone like Washington, who was perpetually in motion, and sometimes there were additional difficulties. Businessman and writer Elkanah Watson related a particular incident involving the painter and sculptor Joseph Wright.

As Washington told it (according to Watson): "Wright came to Mount Vernon with the singular request that I should permit him to take a model of my face, in plaster of Paris, to which I consented, with some reluctance. He oiled my features over; and placing me flat upon my back, upon a cot, preceded to daub my face with the plaster. Whilst in this ludicrous attitude, Mrs. Washington entered the room; and seeing my face thus overspread with the plaster, involuntarily exclaimed. Her cry excited me in a disposition to smile, which gave my mouth a slight twist, or compression of the lips that is now observable in the bust which Wright afterward made."[33]

Washington was wise enough to know that the more portraits, sculptures, and books there were about him, the more famous and successful he would be in all his endeavors. Luckily, he had a life partner who understood that as well and made many of these endeavors her own.

CHAPTER 5

GEORGE AND MARTHA: PARTNERS IN LIFE AND BUSINESS

"Portrait of Martha Dandridge Custis"
by John Wollaston (1757)

MOST AMERICANS REVERE MARTHA WASHINGTON AS THE mother of our country. But they can't relate to her as easily as to other founding mothers like Abigail Adams and Dolley Madison, whose lives were more vivid and colorful.

There are even more impediments in getting to know "the real Martha Washington" than there are with her husband. First is the fact, as noted earlier, that she likely burned most of their private correspondence after his death. (Somewhat surprisingly to modern readers, this was the custom for many couples in the eighteenth century.) Those missing letters have left a gap in our intimate knowledge about both of them. But for Martha, who appears to history as a supporting character in the greater drama of her husband's career, the gap is much larger.

Like most women of her day—including among the elites—Martha did not make public statements or write things the public would see. Abigail Adams didn't do so either, but fortunately most of her letters to John have been preserved. At least 1,160 letters between the second U.S. president and his wife are stored in historical archives. By contrast, only three letters between George and Martha Washington are known to exist today.

There is also a gap in our knowledge of Martha's appearance. Most of the portraits that exist today were painted when she was older. The best-known portrait of her was painted by Gilbert Stuart (who also painted George) when she was well into her sixties. In an image that has been compared to "Old Mother Hubbard," she appears plump with snow-white hair in a large cap.

This relative dearth of documentary and visual evidence has made it difficult to imagine what Martha was like in her twenties, during her courtship with George. It has also led to speculation that George married her solely for her wealth while he secretly pined for his friend's wife, Sally Fairfax.[1] But once again, the Washington business archive, including letters, invoices, and receipts—George's as well as Martha's—provides a more complete picture of the real Martha Dandridge Custis Washington. They show a young woman who was lively and vivacious with considerable business acumen.

Much about young Martha's physical appearance and taste in fashion can be ascertained from the purchase orders for clothing that the Washingtons sent to merchants in London. Patricia Brady, author of the 2005 biography *Martha Washington: An American Life*, found that the sizes of Martha's clothes as stated in the purchase orders correspond to those of a slender woman. "Everything they ordered from England refers to her tiny hands, her tiny feet, her small waist, her slim arms," Brady told the *Washington Post*. "When you were buying at a distance like that, you had to be honest. If you said you were slim and they sent you a small dress and you weighed 200 pounds, it would really be a waste of money."[2]

Brady also had the Forensic Anthropology and Computer Enhancement Services (FACES) laboratory at Louisiana State University do a computer-enhanced age regression of one of Martha's middle-age portraits to show what she likely looked like in her twenties. The result is a stunning portrait of a young Martha with brown hair and hazel eyes, adapted from the regression by artist Michael Deas, which now hangs for visitors to see at Mount Vernon.[3]

Like George, Martha also showed a good deal of social ambition, and in this respect they were well matched. Eight months older than George, Martha was born on June 2, 1731, in New Kent County, Virginia, near Williamsburg. She grew up on the Chestnut Grove plantation built by her father, John Dandridge. Dandridge had come to Virginia from England when he was 15 and was most likely the descendant of farmers or craftsmen who were part of the English middle (or "middling") class.[4] Martha's mother, Fanny Jones Dandridge, was a fourth-generation Virginian whom Brady describes as belonging to the "respected landowning gentry," but "not grandees with uncounted acres."[5]

By colonial standards, Chestnut Grove was modest. As Brady writes, "Plantations encompassed everything from estates with thousands of acres, hundreds of slaves, and grand mansions to little more than jumped-up farms where the owners worked in the fields. Chestnut Grove was somewhere in the middle of this range but was still considered genteel."[6] Although New Kent County records were long ago destroyed by fire, Brady estimates that the Dandridges had 15 to 20 slaves, based on the acreage of Chestnut Grove.

As the eldest of eight children, Martha was given many household responsibilities. Since the relatively small number of slaves probably couldn't be spared from the tobacco field, which was the main source of wealth for Chestnut Grove and other Virginia plantations, most of the household tasks had to be performed by family members. Among the many things Martha likely learned to do at her mother's side were gathering eggs from hens, killing and plucking turkeys and chickens, spinning and weaving wool and linen, gathering herbs and roots for home remedies, making soap from lye and grease, salting and smoking meat and fish, and making clothes, towels, sheets, curtains, tablecloths, and mattresses. As Brady writes: "The most common verb from this long list is 'make,' and that's what colonial women did. Small planters purchased a few imported luxuries, but not most of the necessities of daily life."[7]

Colonial families often treated these domestic activities as more important for girls than reading, writing, and arithmetic, and John and Fanny Dandridge likely put these skills at the forefront for their daughters as well. Nevertheless, Martha did learn how to read and write and do basic calculations. She was a reader for the rest of her life, with interests ranging from the Bible to gothic romance novels.[8] Martha's letters, meanwhile, were "short, direct, and to the point" with "no ornamental flourishes, no high-falutin' sentiments [and] no musings on abstract subjects," Brady writes.[9]

Martha's family was deeply involved in the local church, and Martha herself would be a churchgoer and Bible reader all her life. The family attended New Kent County's church of St. Peter's Parish (then affiliated with the Church of England), where her father was a vestryman and churchwarden—leader of the board of laymen who managed the church's finances and activities.[10]

Like many colonial churches, St. Peter's was one of the centers of rural social life. Before and after church,

Brady writes, "neighbors took the opportunity to visit and do business in the churchyard."[11] Invitations would fly for dinners, barbecues, fish frys, and barn dances. Martha—like George a very social young person—would frequently attend these events, plus the balls at nearby Williamsburg, the colony capital and a growing metropolitan town.

Historian Bruce Chadwick writes that these provincial balls were more like socials than the formal debutante balls in which young women were presented. For the most part, those wouldn't come to the United States until the nineteenth century. At the eighteenth-century balls in Williamsburg and other towns, Chadwick writes: "Young women were not formally presented to those invited to the ball . . . They simply attended and were introduced to different people they saw there amid the whirling couples on the dance floor."[12]

It may have been at one of these events in Williamsburg that Martha met Daniel Custis, a wealthy bachelor more than 20 years her senior. Custis' family was one of the richest in Virginia, and indeed in all the American colonies. Unfortunately for the women he courted, Daniel also had a cantankerous father who was suspicious of every prospective bride. John Custis had chased away many young women, including an heiress who would have brought a much bigger dowry than Martha.[13] For months while his son was courting Martha, John Custis would go into a rage when even talking about her. He threatened Daniel with disinheritance and told friends he'd rather throw his silver into the road than let the Dandridge girl enjoy it.[14] (He had a grand house in the center of Williamsburg, where there actually were roads.)

But Martha was confident enough to arrange a meeting to talk to her prospective father-in-law. No one knows what was said in their conversation, but afterward John did a complete reversal and welcomed her into the family.

A confidant of John's wrote to Daniel, who lived separately on the family's plantation in New Kent County, called the White House, of his father's amazing change of heart. The confidant, a Williamsburg attorney named James Power, wrote: "I am empowered by your father to let you know that he heartily and willingly consents to your marriage with Miss Dandridge—that he has so good a character of her, that he had rather you should have her than any lady in Virginia—nay, if possible he is as much enamored with her character as you are with her person, and this is owing chiefly to a prudent speech of her own."[15]

John Custis didn't live to see his son's wedding. He died a few months later in 1749, and Daniel and Martha married the next year at the Dandridges' Chestnut Grove on May 5, 1750. Daniel was then 38 and Martha just shy of 19. Upon his father's death Daniel inherited a vast fortune, including 18,000 acres of prime agricultural land (mostly for growing tobacco), homes in Williamsburg and Jamestown, and nearly 300 slaves.

Daniel and Martha made their home at the White House plantation. Despite her young age, Martha "proved very efficient at creating an orderly household, just as her mother had trained her," Brady writes.[16] The couple filled the house with the latest luxury goods shipped from London. Memorandum books from Daniel show they ordered a variety of items, including satin suits, china dishes, grinding stones, and spices such as nutmeg. They would frequently entertain guests and hold parties.[17]

Martha was soon pregnant and she had four children over five years, two of whom died when they were toddlers. The two who survived were John Parke Custis (nicknamed Jacky) and Martha Parke Custis (nicknamed Patsy). In the summer of 1757, both Jacky and Daniel fell ill with what appears to have been a throat infection and were treated with largely ineffective medicines by a Williamsburg doctor. Jacky survived, but Daniel did not. On July 8, Martha became a widow.[18]

Martha mourned her husband, but she had little time for grief with two small children to raise and a large estate to run. Although she relied on advice and assistance from Daniel's friends and business associates, Martha acted largely as an independent businesswoman—an unusual step for the time. "Ordinarily, an inexperienced young widow might look to her father, brother, or brothers-in-law for assistance," Brady explains. "But her father was a year dead, her husband an only son, and her brothers even less experienced than she."[19]

Martha involved herself in every aspect of Daniel's vast business endeavors, which included "overseeing the harvesting of a large tobacco crop on several plantations and transporting it to seaports for delivery to England; maintaining dozens of teams of horses; managing more than 200 slaves and providing food, clothing and medicine for all of them; plus taking care of her tenant farmers, overseers and her own family."[20] She wrote letters to the overseas merchants Daniel dealt with in London, Liverpool, and Glasgow, informing them of Daniel's death and subtly hinting that she wasn't going to be taken advantage of.

To the London merchant John Hanbury & Company, Martha wrote: "I now enclose the bill of lading for the tobacco which I hope will get safe to your hands, and have reason to believe it is extremely good. I hope you will sell it at a good price. Mr. Custis' estate will be kept together for some time, and I think it will be proper to continue his account in the same manner as if he was living."[21] In another letter, Martha expressed hope to a British merchant that their association would be "agreeable and lasting to us both." Brady writes that the implication that Martha wouldn't hesitate to take her business elsewhere "couldn't be missed" and remarks that Martha "understood financial power and didn't hesitate to use it."[22]

Martha also continued Daniel's practice of lending money at interest to smaller farmers and townsfolk. She kept careful records and even confronted borrowers in default. She once had the horses hitched up and drove into Williamsburg to meet a deadbeat borrower face-to-face "to his shrill and voluble indignation."[23]

Though saddened by Daniel's death and burdened by her new responsibilities, Martha did her best to handle these tasks with joy. As she wrote to a friend, "I have learned from experience that a greater part of our happiness or misery depends upon our disposition, and not upon our circumstances."[24]

Nevertheless, it was the custom in colonial times for widows and widowers to remarry after a brief period. Martha followed this custom with her marriage to George Washington less than two years after Daniel Custis died.

Martha may have wanted a partner to shoulder the burden of negotiation with merchants and debtors. She may have also wanted a surrogate father for her children. Whatever the case, as one of the richest widows in Virginia, she had no shortage of male suitors. In eighteenth-century America, both men and women hunted fortunes when looking for potential spouses, and they made no real secret about it. Newspapers sometimes ran wedding articles that relayed the exact amount of the bride's dowry.[25]

So Martha had good reason to be cautious. She accepted invitations to parties and entertained at the White House, but she was careful about entering into a relationship with many of the men she met. A year after John's death, she was still weighing the merits of two serious suitors. One was Charles Carter, whose family was from the same upper stratum of Virginia's plantation elite as the Custises. The other was an ambitious soldier and entrepreneur who didn't have nearly the resources of Carter, but who clearly had ambition, drive, and many plans for his future success.

There is much we do not know about George and Martha's courtship. Their correspondence from the late 1750s is lost to history, as it was likely among the letters that were burned after Washington's death. Writes Brady: "Of all the letters that Martha and George Washington wrote to each other over the years, the destruction of the correspondence of the spring of 1758 is most distressing. We have no idea of the tone, sentiments, or frequency of those courtship letters as the young couple moved closer to a decision to marry."[26] We can't even be sure of where the couple actually met.

But a few things can still be surmised. Carter, though wealthy and apparently of fine character according to the letters of his friends, was nearing 50 and already had 12 children by his late wife. Martha may not have wanted to take on the raising of such a large family in addition to her own. And George, eight months younger than she was, offered youth, energy, passion—and burgeoning fame.

When he met Martha in 1758, George Washington was already to some degree an international celebrity. Five years earlier, at the age of 20, Washington had enlisted in Virginia's militia. The Virginia Regiment, as it was called, was formed by Robert Dinwiddie, a British colonial administrator. This force would aid the British in defending the colony against foreign aggression. In February 1753, Dinwiddie—likely impressed by Washington's reputation as a diligent surveyor of rough wilderness terrain—promoted him to the rank of major and sent him on a mission to communicate British concerns to the French settlements that had popped up in what is now northern Pennsylvania.

Washington and his small party—which included frontier explorer Christopher Gist and some American Indians who knew the region—traveled 1,000 miles round-trip from Virginia by foot, horse, raft, and canoe to a French fort in the Ohio River Valley. Washington successfully delivered the message and told the French commander that the British wanted the settlers to leave the region immediately. The commander rejected this request, but in a polite manner, and he even showed Washington and his party some hospitality. Nevertheless, when Washington returned with news of the rejection, the British-appointed Governor's Council authorized Dinwiddie to raise a force and attack, and the nine-year French and Indian War was on.

As the war began in 1754, Dinwiddie asked Washington to prepare a report on his travels for Virginia's House of Burgesses. Using notes from a journal he had kept, Washington vividly described the wilderness terrain and rough weather that he and his party traveled through. One passage reads: "At 11 o'Clock we set out for the Fort; and were prevented from arriving there 'til the 11th by excessive Rains, Snows, and bad Travelling, through many Mires and Swamps, which we were obliged to pass, to avoid crossing the Creek, which was impossible, either by fording or rafting, the Water was so high and rapid."[27]

Dinwiddie was so impressed with George's journal that he circulated it far and wide, as did others, until it became almost the equivalent of a modern bestseller. *The Journal of Major George Washington*, as it was entitled, was published and distributed throughout the colonies and in Great Britain. It was also serialized in several newspapers. Historian Hayes argues that the work "deserves recognition as a major contribution" to American travel writing.[28]

This fame brought George a swift promotion. In 1755, Dinwiddie appointed him colonel and commander of Virginia's military forces. Washington had hoped his advancement in the Virginia militia would lead to his being given a commission as a "regular" officer in the British military. He traveled to Boston to appeal directly to British commander William Shirley for such a post but was turned down.[29] So by 1758, at the age of 26, Washington was winding down his military career and preparing for a domestic life at Mount Vernon as a farmer and businessman.

By this time, Washington was looking for a wife, and Martha provided what he needed, not only in terms of wealth but in personal and practical companionship. As historian Lengel relayed to the *Washington Post*, "She was a physically attractive woman, an excellent manager, poised and self-possessed. George felt he could rely on her both to be a partner in his business endeavors and"—while he was away—"to manage the family, the estate, financial affairs, political affairs, even."[30]

As for how Martha viewed George, Brady writes: "She discovered an honorable gentleman who would never embarrass her, a kind man who would love the children, hers and theirs [although they would never have any biological children together], a man faithful to his word who would safeguard the Custis inheritance. His lack of fortune needn't have concerned her since she had plenty of money for them both. She was also a woman confident of her own allure, unafraid of rivals for his affection. In George Washington, she saw a man with whom she believed she could live lovingly and happily. And she was right."[31]

George Washington married Martha Dandridge Custis on January 6, 1759, at the Custis family's White House plantation. George, Martha, and the children stayed there and around Williamsburg for almost three more months. Then on April 2 of that year, they loaded a heavy coach with items from the Custis estate—everything from cheeses to a mahogany desk to bedroom curtains—and began the four-day journey 125 miles upstate to their new home, Mount Vernon.

There are two common misconceptions about Mount Vernon. One is that George Washington was born there. The other, conflicting with the first, is that he built the estate from the ground up. Neither is true, but these widespread beliefs are testament to the fact that Washington loved Mount Vernon and left an imprint on the landscape that remains to this day.

But it was far from certain that Mount Vernon would ever belong to him, or that once it did, he would make it his primary residence. Unfortunately, it took the tragic death of three people Washington loved to make Mount Vernon his.

As previously discussed, Augustine had left Mount Vernon to George's older brother, Lawrence, who died in 1752. Lawrence left Mount Vernon to his wife, Anne, but she would soon remarry and move away from the estate. George struck a deal with Anne by which he would lease Mount Vernon from her and keep the revenues he raised from farming the land. When Anne died in 1761, leaving no heir (the couple's only child had died seven years earlier), per Lawrence's will, George became the owner of Mount Vernon.[32]

Meanwhile, the question must have arisen for George and Martha as to whether it wasn't more practical to remain at the Custis plantation. George had more than 5,550 acres under his control at Mount Vernon from his inheritance and adjoining land he purchased.[33] But that wasn't anywhere close to the 18,000 acres Martha and her children received from Daniel's estate. Further, the Custis land yielded far more of the prized tobacco crop. As Brady writes, "The growing season was longer there, the soil richer and better suited to tobacco, trade with Great Britain far more convenient."[34]

But since he was a boy, Washington had dreamed of having Mount Vernon as his own. His happiest boyhood memories were there, and throughout his life he always longed for it whenever military or political affairs took him away. As president living in the glorious executive mansion in the then–U.S. capital of Philadelphia, Washington would write wistfully of Mount Vernon to British agriculturalist Arthur Young. "No estate in United America is more pleasantly situated than this," Washington declared. "It lyes in a high, dry & healthy country, 300 miles by water from the Sea—and, as you will see by the plan, on one of the finest Rivers in the world."[35]

It's true that in that oft-quoted letter to Young, Washington—ever the entrepreneur—was touting Mount Vernon's qualities so Young would spread the word that some parts of the estate were available for rent. But the words capture Washington's love of Mount Vernon and his dedication to improving it over his lifetime. The river Washington referred to is of course the Potomac, which he and others spent much effort trying to make more navigable.

Martha had never traveled more than 20 miles past the New Kent County house she was born in. But she wasn't going to stand in the way of George's dreams. So George—who per Virginia law was in control of Martha's share of the Custis land and that of the children until they reached adulthood—rented out the White House plantation before they moved.

There was another reason to settle at Mount Vernon. George had his eye on representing the area around Mount Vernon in Virginia's House of Burgesses. Though limited in power by the colony's royal governor, the burgesses had a say in Virginia's internal affairs. It was also a chance to meet other planters and learned men like Thomas Jefferson and Patrick Henry, who would be his future allies in the independence movement. Washington had been elected to represent Frederick County— encompassing the Shenandoah Valley area where he spent much time both as a surveyor and during the French and Indian War—in 1758. In 1761, after he and Martha settled in at Mount Vernon, he would be elected to represent Fairfax County and would continue as a burgess until 1775, when he took command of the Continental Army.

* * *

Visitors to Mount Vernon today marvel at the beauty of its lawn and gardens and the glamour of its "Mansion House," where the Washington family lived. They are mostly seeing Mount Vernon as it looked in 1799, a tribute to the Mount Vernon Ladies' Association, whose longtime goal has been to preserve Washington's home as it was when he died. Forty years earlier, however, when George and Martha first arrived, the estate was very much a work in progress.

When Washington first leased Mount Vernon, the Mansion House, which has stood at almost 11,000 square feet since the 1790s, was likely just around 3,500 square feet.[36] The home's first expansion was conducted while Washington was away fighting the French and Indian War. The construction was directed by his neighbor William Fairfax, a carpenter, and a farm overseer. The work itself was mostly performed by Washington's enslaved labor force.[37]

The plan was to build a full second story and some extra rooms on the main floor. But that expansion still wasn't quite finished when Martha and the children arrived. As Chadwick describes it: "The dark wooden bannister on the new, two-story staircase had not been completely installed and the painting of the interior walls of the home remained unfinished because the painter left and stole all of Washington's paint mixture. Washington's lengthy absences had contributed to the disrepair at Mount Vernon, but he also blamed the workers and plantation managers for ignoring the upkeep of the home."[38]

Renovations continued, and George and Martha also ordered many luxury items from London to spruce up Mount Vernon. These included carpets made with fine wool, curtains festooned with graceful curves, and cloth-covered cornices to put atop windows.[39] Jacky and Patsy received English toys, dolls, books, and musical instruments.

Coming as they did from modest backgrounds, George and Martha did watch their finances carefully and constantly negotiated for the best prices. Chadwick notes that when Martha sent an order for goods to London, she often "stipulated that the buyers should not purchase the most expensive types, but look for cheaper ones."[40] In one order, she requested that the merchants find her an elegant lace dress with ruffles, cap, and a handkerchief "not to exceed" 40 British pounds, and a necklace and earrings "not to exceed" 7 pounds in currency.[41]

Chadwick points out that "Martha and her husband were usually happy with orders from London, but they complained loudly when they received damaged goods or when purchases were missing." George and Martha both signed a stern letter in 1772 complaining about the price and quality of clothing sent from London for a then-teenage Patsy. They said that the London store overcharged for the dress and did not send the cap and fur scarf that had been promised. They added that the five caps they ordered separately could have been bought in the colonies "at much less price."[42]

Sometimes George would take even more drastic action when he felt he was being taken advantage of. When several items were missing from another order for Patsy, her stepfather stopped the ship from leaving and searched it high and low. Disappointingly, he still could not find the items that Patsy longed for.[43]

But the most radical action he took with regard to British merchants whom he thought were shortchanging him came in response to the lower-than-expected prices he was getting for tobacco. This led him to get rid of Mount Vernon's tobacco crop altogether and replace it with foodstuffs. He influenced other farmers along the way—and ultimately helped start a revolution.

CHAPTER 6

WASHINGTON'S GREEN THUMB: THE FIELDS AND ORCHARDS OF MOUNT VERNON

Dried Hemp Today at Mount Vernon

Photo by Kristen H. Murray

WASHINGTON'S INHERITANCE IN COMBINATION WITH AD-
joining land that he had purchased made for a sizable
estate of more than 5,500 acres. Tobacco was the primary
crop of Mount Vernon, as it was of many of the larger
farms of Virginia of the day, including the Custis plantation that Martha had managed after her first husband's
death. It was 1759, and it looked like George Washington
was set for a prosperous, quiet, yet somewhat dull life as a
Virginia "gentleman farmer."

But as Woodrow Wilson notes in his biography of
Washington, tobacco farmers still had to prepare for the
worst. "Virginia wealth was not to be counted till crops
were harvested and got to market," Wilson writes. "The
current price of tobacco might leave you with or without a balance to your credit in London, your only clear-
inghouse, as it chanced . . . Both what you sold and what
you bought must take the hazards of the sea voyage, the
whims of sea captains, the chances of a foreign market."[1]

By this time, both George and Martha had seen
enough tragedies and reversals of fortune in their own
lives. They weren't afraid to make major changes in their
way of life to guard against headwinds or ensure long-
term prosperity.

Martha's letters show her shrewdly negotiating on the
prices of tobacco she would sell to London merchants as
well as the luxury goods, such as silk, that she would buy
from them.[2] Washington likely learned much from his
new wife about bargaining with merchants.

At Mount Vernon, Martha would also prove "an energetic and effective household manager," Lengel notes.[3] Martha oversaw most things domestic. George and the Mount Vernon workforce would farm the fields, but Martha was in charge of food production for the family and the workforce. This included arduous tasks like overseeing the gathering of milk from the cows at the Mount Vernon dairy and the cutting of cattle carcasses to be taken to the Mount Vernon smokehouse for curing. During the winter "hog season," Martha would supervise the dismembering of the slain hogs sent to her by George and his men. As Chadwick describes it, this involved "working with her domestics to chop the animal into pieces, dipping the ham shoulder and flanks into brine, processing the fat into lard, and stuffing the intestines with sausage."[4]

Martha would almost always walk around with several keys to the buildings at Mount Vernon and rooms at the Mansion House in case something needed to be taken care of. George could make a day trip to Alexandria to oversee the shipping of Mount Vernon's tobacco and other goods from the port city with confidence that Martha could manage the day-to-day operations of the farm.[5] Later on, when Washington was gone for extended absences at meetings of the Continental Congress and then in command of American forces during the war, he would hire overseers, but Martha would always retain a strong say in the estate's operations.

Washington's entrepreneurial instincts were on full display in his early decision to abandon tobacco for wheat, a decision he made based on a combination of observation, research, and remarkable foresight.

Tobacco from the American colonies was in high

demand in England, where residents snapped up cigars and the finely ground chewing tobacco called "snuff" at a high rate. By the mid-eighteenth century, a large tobacco crop could facilitate for an American farmer a line of credit with merchants in Britain. Since colonies were mostly barred by Britain from creating their own money, tobacco warehouse receipts, or "tobacco notes" as they were called, functioned as a substitute currency.[6]

When farmers imported goods from British merchants, they would draw upon their credit from the supply of tobacco they had sent to the merchants that year. Growing tobacco, as opposed to other crops, was also a symbol of a landowner's status, and those who grew it were often called "planters" rather than "farmers" as a badge of distinction.

With Martha's assistance, George was mastering the intricacies of marketing tobacco. She put him in touch with Robert Cary & Company, the London mercantile firm that was the middleman in selling the Custis estate's tobacco in Great Britain. The Cary firm became the London agent in selling tobacco from Mount Vernon as well.

However, Washington soon began to see the shortcomings of the tobacco trade as well as the trouble that loomed on the horizon. Washington had the foresight to realize that despite the social standing that growing tobacco gave them, Mount Vernon needed to diversify its crops and operations to survive. By the 1760s, so many American farmers were growing tobacco that there was an oversupply on the world market. As a result, prices were falling, and in the case of some nonpremium tobacco, tumbling.

In his letters to Cary, Washington frequently expressed frustration that his crop wasn't fetching a higher price despite the improvement he was making in its cultivation. It was becoming what economists call a "buyer's market," and the reputation of a particular plantation didn't matter that much, as planters hadn't found a way to "brand" their particular product. Washington wrote Cary in 1762 complaining of the "lowness of the price" his tobacco fetched in Great Britain and wondering aloud if it was "an Art beyond my skill, to succeed in making good Tobo [tobacco]." Washington explained with consternation, "I have used my utmost endeavours for that purpose this two or 3 years past—& am once again urged to express my surprize at finding that I do not partake of the best prices that are going."[7]

There were also specific burdens that American tobacco growers faced in dealing with their mother country. Shipping carried insurance and freight costs, as well as the risk of the ship being attacked by pirates or a foreign power. There were British duties on goods exported from the colonies, which would eventually be one of the causes of the colonies' rebellion. Then there were the fees farmers had to pay Cary and other middlemen.

On top of this, tobacco was harming Mount Vernon soil, making it more difficult to replant tobacco or grow other crops. Today, it's an established scientific fact that tobacco depletes nutrients in soil more rapidly than other crops.[8] But Washington came to this conclusion by observing the fields at Mount Vernon and by reading the latest theories in books, which he routinely ordered from England, including Batty Langley's *New Principles of*

Gardening, Thomas Hale's *A Compleat Book of Husbandry*, and *A New System of Agriculture; Or, A Plain, Easy, and Demonstrative Method of Speedily Growing Rich*, authored by an unnamed "Country Gentleman."[9]

Ultimately, Washington's observations led him to phase out tobacco and replace it with whatever crops and services the market demanded. It was the first step toward making Mount Vernon what historian Harlow Giles Unger calls "a diversified agroindustrial enterprise."[10]

Washington had observed the practices of some smaller farms in Virginia and noticed they were growing different types of wheat. Scotch-Irish and German immigrants who had recently migrated to Virginia and other colonies had brought several varieties of wheat from their native lands. Other small-scale farmers in the region had also joined in.[11] Seeing the advantages of wheat as a crop—including reduced harm to the soil and a growing domestic market for foodstuff as the American population was increasing—Washington decided to make Mount Vernon one of the first big farms in Virginia to grow wheat as its primary crop.

The changeover in the early 1760s was small at first, as Washington needed to change a variety of farming practices to ensure the most successful cultivation. Then, in the middle of the decade, Washington dramatically picked up the pace. In 1764, Mount Vernon produced 257 bushels of wheat; in 1766, 2,331 bushels, and by 1769, 6,241 bushels.[12] An inveterate experimentalist with a passion for variety, he also planted different strains in order to see which ones did best in the Virginia climate, including summer wheat, red-straw wheat, lamas wheat, double-headed wheat, yellow-bearded wheat, early wheat, and Russian wheat.[13]

Meanwhile, tobacco was rapidly disappearing from Washington's holdings. By 1766, he had ceased growing tobacco at Mount Vernon, though until the 1770s he would continue to grow a small amount on the Custis lands that Martha and the children had inherited.[14]

Explaining in a letter to Cary in 1765 why he was phasing out tobacco, Washington wrote: "It appears pretty evident to me from the prices I have generally got for my Tobacco in London, & from some other concomitant Circumstances, that it only suits the Interest of a few particular Gentlemen to continue their consignments of this commodity to that place, while others shoud endeavour to substitute some other Article in place of Tobacco, and try their success therewith."[15]

He also asked Cary's advice regarding a new crop the agro-entrepreneur planned to cultivate. "You woud do me a singular favour in advising of the general price one might expect for good Hemp."[16]

※ ※ ※

Today, the name Jethro Tull is most likely to mean something to those familiar with the British rock band formed in the late 1960s. But the band's namesake was an actual historical figure—a pioneering eighteenth-century agronomist who was greatly admired in his time, including by Washington. Tull (a British viscount) was a noted inventor who developed new machines and growing methods that would revolutionize British farming.

Washington started reading Tull's agricultural manual

Horse-Hoeing Husbandry when considering what crops to grow to replace tobacco. According to Hayes, Washington, who would frequently copy out book passages that he thought could be of later use, "transcribed Tull's discussions of wheat and hemp at considerable length."[17]

Hemp, of course, stems from the same species as cannabis, and ever since it became widely known that Washington grew hemp, there has been speculation that he and/or his associates may have partaken of the substance for either medicinal or recreational purposes. However, exhaustive searches have found no evidence that Washington either smoked hemp or grew it for that purpose. Hemp had (and still has) widespread industrial uses. It was utilized to make clothing, rope, mattress and pillow covers, and bags.

Washington briefly considered making hemp his primary crop before settling on wheat. But he would still grow it throughout his life, mostly for use around Mount Vernon. Uses included the making of rope, canvas, and thread, as well as the giant nets utilized in Mount Vernon's fishery.[18]

In 1794, about five years into his presidency, Washington wrote one of his detailed instructional letters to his then–farm manager, William Pearce:

> I am very glad to hear that the Gardener has saved
> so much of the St foin seed, & that of the India Hemp.
> Make the most you can of both, by sowing them again
> in drills. Where to sow the first I am a little at a loss
> (as Hares are very destructive to it) but think, as the
> Lucern which was sown broad in the Inclosure by the

Spring, has come to nothing; as the ground is good; and probably as free from Hares as any other place, it might as well be put there; as I am very desirous of getting into a full stock of seed as soon as possible. Let the ground be well prepared, and the Seed (St foin) be sown in April. The Hemp may be sown any where.[19]

Though wheat became Washington's primary crop, he wanted never again to be dependent on one crop as he had been (and as many plantations still were) on tobacco. At one time in the 1780s, he was raising in the fields of Mount Vernon barley, clover, corn, carrots, cabbage, flax, millet, oats, orchard grass, peas, potatoes, pumpkins, rye, spelt, turnips, timothy, and wheat. All told, the number of crops he grew, attempted to grow, or experimented with totaled more than 60.

From Tull and other English agriculturalists like Arthur Young, with whom he corresponded extensively, Washington kept up to date on the latest farming machinery and techniques. In particular, he learned how to preserve Mount Vernon's soil through experimenting with different types of fertilizer, plowing, and crop rotation.

Washington was particularly fascinated by different types of manure and their specific properties. For a farmer, Washington joked in a letter to George William Fairfax, manure was the "first transmutation towards gold."[20]

To store this "gold," Washington built what he called a "dung repository," which has recently been reconstructed at Mount Vernon. Just after he and Martha arrived at the Constitutional Convention in Philadelphia in May 1787, Washington penned a letter to his nephew and then–farm manager George Augustine Washington instructing him how to build the repository. After directing that it be built at the "mouth of the drain by the [horse] Stable," presumably to make it easier to collect the horse manure, Washington told his nephew to line the bottom with "good clay" and "ram it well before you pave it." This must be done, Washington explained, "to prevent the liquid manure from sinking, and thereby being lost."[21]

He also told his nephew to get assistance from Cornelius, a stonemason and bricklayer from Ireland who had worked for two years as an indentured servant at Mount Vernon. Cornelius then entered into a contract with Washington to work there for another year for room and board and a salary.[22] Enslaved workers likely helped out as well.

Washington had been experimenting with manure for decades. As a young farmer just starting out, he would mix manure with other waste products in order to determine which combination made the best formula. He would use a large wooden box with ten compartments for these experiments, and, like any good scientist, he would keep careful records. In a diary entry from 1760, Washington described how he "Mixd my Composts in a box," taking "a Peck of Horse Dung" for one compartment, and in the others used "mud taken out of the Creek," along with cow dung, sheep dung, and other earthen materials.[23] He then planted inside the box (which must have been pretty big) three grains each of wheat, oats, and barley, all at equal distances in Rows & of equal depth." In this particular experiment, conducted over a month, the sheep manure seemed to work best.[24]

Washington and his workers would conduct many

more such experiments throughout his life. In 1796, he wrote to his farm manager William Pearce instructing him to have the workers "scrape up all the trash, of every sort & kind about the houses, & in holes & corners and throw it" into the dung repository to mix with the manure.[25]

Washington's singular focus on soil conservation and replenishment stood in sharp contrast to other large-scale farmers of the day. Land was still so plentiful at the time that, as Jefferson would note in a letter to Washington in 1793, Virginia farmers "can buy an acre of new land cheaper than we can manure an old one."[26]

As pioneering agricultural historian Paul Leland Haworth explained in his 1915 book, *George Washington: Farmer*: "It was this cheapness of land that made it almost impossible for the Virginians to break away from their ruinous system—ruinous, not necessarily to themselves, but to future generations. Conservation was then a doctrine that was little preached. Posterity could take care of itself. Only a few persons like Washington realized their duty to the future."[27]

Washington knew that the trend of simply replacing farmed-out land with cheaper land couldn't go on either at Mount Vernon or at other farms. So he practiced— and preached—the wise use of land and its conservation for future years and future generations. As president in 1791, Washington wrote to British agriculturalist Arthur Young that Americans should emulate the methods farmers were using in Britain.

"A farmer in England, where land is dear and labor cheap, finds it his interest to improve and cultivate highly, that he may reap large crops from a small quantity of ground." In America, by contrast, "the aim of the farmers in this Country (if they can be called farmers) is not to make the most they can from the land, which is, or has been cheap, but the most of the labor, which is dear, the consequence of which has been, much ground has been *scratched* over and none cultivated or improved as it ought to have been." He also expressed optimism that Americans' attitudes about conservation were changing by "pretty rapid strides."[28]

Agriculture experts still look to Washington's scientific farming practices today. The *National Geographic* magazine recently called Washington "America's first composter."[29] Hugh Hammond Bennett, who is considered the father of modern soil conservation, cited Washington as a pioneer in this arena. In a 1933 speech at Ohio State University—during the period of drought known as the American Dust Bowl—Bennett pointed to Washington's crop rotation, cessation of planting tobacco, and decision to plant clover, which enriches soil, as early efforts "to check erosion." He noted that Mount Vernon still had "venerable cedars and oaks" from Washington's time.[30]

Eighty-five years after Bennett's speech—and some 220 years after Washington's death—crops are still harvested from the Mount Vernon soil, and some venerable trees from Washington's time still stand. Indeed, he supervised the planting and growing of all kinds of trees over his lifetime.

* * *

The legendary Johnny Appleseed was in fact a real man named John Chapman who planted numerous apple orchards in Pennsylvania, Ohio, Illinois, and what is now West Virginia. Contrary to legend, however, Chapman was not a vagrant or drifter but a savvy entrepreneur who was one of America's first real estate entrepreneurs.

Beginning in the 1790s, speculators who had bought land in what was then the western frontier of the United States (now the Midwest) were having trouble unloading it. So they offered prospective settlers a deal: if they planted 50 apple trees and 20 peach trees within three years, they would be granted 100 acres. Chapman had the bright idea to pick a spot, plant the trees, acquire the deed, then "flip" the property by selling it to other settlers. He would then head further west and start the process all over again.[31]

In similar fashion, Washington also planted many trees at Mount Vernon, both to improve the landscape and turn a profit.

As mentioned earlier, when Washington was a teenage surveyor in Virginia's Shenandoah Valley, he wrote in his journal, "We went through most beautiful Groves of Sugar Trees [known today as sugar maples] & spent the best part of the Day in admiring the Trees & richness of the Land." As architecture historian Joseph Manca writes, "The notion of the 'richness of the land' expressed here was an aesthetic reaction but also an observation of the future economic possibilities of the land for farming."[32]

Washington would in time acquire much land in the Shenandoah Valley and would also plant sugar maples at Mount Vernon. However, he was ultimately more successful with other types of trees.[33]

For instance, at the edge of his farms at Mount Vernon,

Washington designed fruit orchards. Here his crew would plant trees to grow apples, pears, peaches, apricots, and cherries, utilizing a French method called *espalier*. Sometimes called "the Frenchman's bonsai," espalier entails planting trees so that they grow in confined spaces, such as along a fence or wall. Washington would have his gardeners plant many of his peach, apricot, and cherry trees right next to the brick wall.[34] (Espalier is now used to grow trees in America and around the world, everywhere from grand estates to tight urban spaces, where it may be the only way to grow trees in such a dense area of land.) A visitor to Mount Vernon in 1782 marveled at the "immense, extremely well-cultivated" gardens and orchards and commented, "the choicest fruits in the country are to be found there."[35]

But there were some fruits that couldn't be grown in the Northern Virginia climate. So as previously mentioned, Washington—whose taste for variety in all things agricultural bordered on mania—erected a greenhouse. There he planted citrus trees that grew oranges and lemons, which he had previously ordered from merchants. The greenhouse also became a showcase for rare and unusual plants from around the world, including an aloe vera from North Africa and a sago palm from the East Indies.[36]

Even when he was at war, the trees of Mount Vernon were never far from Washington's thoughts. Here are some detailed planting instructions that he wrote from the battlefields of New York in August 1776 to his cousin Lund Washington, who was then managing the estate:

Plant Trees in the room of all dead ones in proper time this Fall. and as I mean to have groves of Trees at each end of the dwelling House, that at the South end to range in a line from the South East Corner to Colo. Fairfax's [adjoining Belvoir estate], extending as low as another line from the Stable to the dry well, and towards the Coach House, Hen House, & Smoak House as far as it can go for a Lane to be left for Carriages to pass to, & from the Stable and Wharf . . .

[T]hese Trees to be Planted without any order or regularity (but pretty thick, as they can at any time be thin'd) and to consist that at the North end, of locusts altogether. & that at the South, of all the clever kind of Trees (especially flowering ones) that can be got, such as Crab apple, Poplar, Dogwood, Sasafras, Lawrel, Willow (especially yellow & Weeping Willow, twigs of which may be got from Philadelphia) and many others which I do not recollect at present—these to be interspersed here and there with ever greens such as Holly, Pine, and Cedar, also Ivy—to these may be added the Wild flowering Shrubs of the larger kind, such as the fringe Tree & several other kinds that might be mentioned.[37]

Washington mentions here that he had picked up some willow twigs in Philadelphia. This was a habit of his. In many of the places he went, Washington would pick up seeds, plants, or young trees in order to have them planted at Mount Vernon. Visitors to the estate would also frequently bring seeds as gifts. Washington wasn't always successful at growing these trees or crops at Mount Vernon. Sometimes the soil just wasn't suited for it. But he was always looking to expand the gardens and orchards there. And as we have already noted, he had a passion for variety and sought to make Mount Vernon a microcosm of America's—and indeed the world's—natural abundance.

Today at Mount Vernon there are many descendants of trees from George Washington's day—and even a few originals. If you so desire, you can even plant descendants of Washington's trees in your own garden, as every spring, Mount Vernon holds a Historic Plant and Garden Sale.

CHAPTER 7

WASHINGTON'S MOUNT VERNON: THE MAKING OF AN INDUSTRIAL VILLAGE

A Camel at Mount Vernon to Commemorate the Original that Washington Had Imported

Photo by Kristen H. Murray

From an early age, Washington's interest in animals paralleled his interest in the different varieties of plants, trees, and crops. In his lifetime, Washington saw a lion, sea lion, elephant, and possibly a tiger. He also brought a camel and an Arabian horse temporarily to Mount Vernon. Nor was his experimental tinkering limited to machinery and crops. He took such a keen interest in animal husbandry and breeding that he became widely known in his own time as the "father" of the American mule.

Throughout his life, Washington attended fairs that featured exotic animals. In 1766, the meticulous Washington recorded paying ten shillings to see a "lyoness," probably at a fair in Alexandria.[1] Three years later, he recorded a payment to see a "tyger," which, as Mount Vernon historian Mary Thompson notes, "could have been either the now-familiar striped Asian tiger or a North American cougar or puma, referred to by the colonists as 'red tigers.'"[2] Washington did see a "cugar" during his presidency in the nation's then-capital of Philadelphia. He was also privileged to see an elephant and a "sea leopard," a type of sea lion.[3]

It was highly unusual for even the most privileged colonial American to see such a variety of African and Asian animals, as zoos were then unknown. The London Zoo was built for scientists in the 1820s and wasn't open to the public until 1847. The first American zoo, the Philadelphia Zoological Gardens, didn't open its doors until 1874. So it required considerable effort for an individual like Washington to see these animals at different traveling exhibitions.

An animal even more rarely sighted in colonial America was the Middle Eastern camel. There are only a handful of recorded instances of Americans importing camels in the eighteenth century.[4] George Washington is the most prominent example. In the Christmas season of 1787, Washington paid to bring a camel to entertain his workers and guests at Mount Vernon. To commemorate this event, every December, Mount Vernon brings a camel named Aladdin onto the grounds.[5]

✳ ✳ ✳

Horses were a necessity in eighteenth-century America, and Washington's skill at riding, caring for, and breeding them was well known to his neighbors and friends. Thomas Jefferson called him "the best horseman of the age and the most graceful."[6]

Riding was a major part of Washington's daily routine at Mount Vernon from the 1760s until shortly before his death in 1799. Every morning after a light breakfast, Washington would climb onto his horse and ride around to inspect the different farms on the estate. He would view how crops were growing, what needed repair, and other details of his operations. Lengel notes that "a typical day's circuit" took Washington around ten miles.[7] This is probably one of the reasons why he usually rode at a canter. "For he liked to ride quickly," noted James Thomas Flexner in *Washington: The Indispensable Man*.[8]

Washington also took long rides as a young surveyor, dashed through the forest on fox hunts, and, of course, rode into battle during wartime. So he knew a good stallion or mare when he saw one, and he applied this experienced eye to the science of breeding. After the tragic death of his stepson John Parke Custis from "camp fever" (probably typhus), caught on the battlefield as one of the general's aides, Washington bought a handsome Arabian horse from Custis' estate. Washington wrote about the horse in his diary in glowing terms. Magnolio was "a chesnut colour, near sixteen hands high, finely formed, and thought by all who have seen him to be perfect," Washington noted in 1785.[9]

Washington first sold Magnolio's services as a stud to nearby owners who wanted to start a breed. Then in 1788 he struck a deal with his neighbor Harry Lee, known as "Light Horse Harry" for his excellent horsemanship as well as his heroism during the Revolutionary War, to trade Magnolio in exchange for 5,000 acres of land in the Kentucky territory.[10] This proved to be a good trade for Washington as the land contained valuable deposits of iron ore.[11]

Washington's excellent horsemanship didn't just stem from natural ability or even from experience. As with many of his other skills, he refined his horsemanship through constant reading about the care and handling of horses. According to Hayes, Washington read "how-to" horsemanship books such as British horse surgeon William Gibson's *New Treatise on the Diseases of Horses* and *The Complete Horseman, or, Perfect Farrier* by Jacques Labessie de Solleysel. Solleysel was a leading authority on all aspects of horse riding and care who taught horsemanship to French nobility. Hayes writes that in addition to the latest methods of treating sick horses, Solleysel's book imparts much knowledge about the "art of riding," including "the rider's proper position, the use of the spur, and the way to execute the movements of dressage." The presence of this book in Washington's library, Hayes concludes, indicates that Washington sought out books to learn "how to ride more effectively—and more elegantly."[12]

Washington's long absence during the Revolutionary War took a toll on Mount Vernon and the family's finances. His cousin Lund had done a competent job with the estate's basic operations, but there were definite areas of neglect. When Washington came home after retiring as general in 1783, he saw "peeling paint, rotten wood, dilapidated outbuildings, broken tools, [and] disordered gardens and fields," writes Lengel.[13]

Also draining the Washingtons' income and assets were the constant stream of visitors, many of whom were simply fans and well-wishers. George and Martha didn't have the heart to turn them away and would give food and lodging to practically anyone, including perfect strangers who showed up on their doorstep.[14]

All this came at a time when there were increased family obligations. George and Martha were raising their two youngest grandchildren—children of the late John Parke Custis—at Mount Vernon. They were also guardians of the two sons of George's late brother Samuel.[15]

So when opportunities arose to import some fine animal breeds from Europe, Washington took advantage of them, eyeing a new stream of income from the business of breeding.

The closest international friendship Washington made during the war was with the young Marquis de Lafayette. Orphaned but wealthy, Lafayette was 19 when the

American colonies declared their independence from Great Britain. Sympathetic to the American cause, he traveled to the United States the next year and persuaded some French officers to come with him. Once here, he volunteered his services to Washington's Continental Army. In appreciation for that gesture—and because he came from the highest ranks of the French nobility—Congress commissioned him a major general.

Lafayette served with Washington at Valley Forge and helped foil an attempt by senior officers to oust him as commander of the military. He also used his contacts in France to aid the Americans with troops and supplies.

Washington and Lafayette grew close, and the bond they developed was almost like a father-son relationship. Lafayette would name his son Georges Washington Louis Gilbert de Lafayette and stay in contact with Washington for the rest of Washington's life.

In 1785, Lafayette received a letter from Washington with what may have seemed like an unusual request: a few hunting hounds that belonged to the king of France. Dogs from the royal kennel were not easy to come by, but Lafayette was eventually able to get his hands on seven large French hounds, which he shipped to the United States, where Washington carefully bred them with the largest of his American-born hounds.[16]

The experiments were successful, and the American Kennel Club now credits Washington with creating a new breed of dog—the American Foxhound—indirectly spurring other hound breeds between the time he resigned as general and became our first president.[17]

But Washington wasn't done. In 1784, Washington

hosted Lafayette for several days at Mount Vernon, and in one of their conversations the Frenchman told him about the large mules belonging to King Charles III that he had seen on a recent visit to Spain. Washington had long been interested in mules, as he had read that they do more work and eat less food than horses. There were some mules in America at the time, but they were too small to pull heavy wagons and other farm equipment.

Mule breeding is difficult, because a mule is a cross between a male donkey (jackass) and a female horse (mare). Moreover, they are almost always sterile, so they can't reproduce on their own. Every new generation of mules requires the mating of a jackass and a mare.

Lafayette promised that he would personally prevail on the king to send Washington a Spanish jackass to breed with the mares at Mount Vernon.[18] Though Spain had a strict prohibition of the exportation of large farm animals, Lafayette and others were eventually able to persuade the king to send Washington two jackasses as a gesture of friendship for the new American nation.[19]

One of the jackasses died on the trip. When the other arrived, Washington named him—appropriately—Royal Gift. Washington sent Mount Vernon overseer John Fairfax, a distant relative of Washington's former neighbors, to Boston to meet Royal Gift and the Spanish handler who would ride him to Virginia. Washington was so concerned that the jackass arrive in good health that he instructed Fairfax and Royal Gift's handler to take plenty of rest breaks, cover the donkey with blankets, and travel no more than 15 miles a day. As a result, it took Royal Gift almost a month to arrive at Mount Vernon.[20]

At first, Royal Gift was stubborn and very slow to reproduce. Washington joked in a letter to his nephew Bushrod Washington that the jackass was "too full of Royalty, to have any thing to do with a plebian race."[21] But then Washington thought of a way to get Royal Gift to do his royal duty. Washington instructed Royal Gift's handler to place two female donkeys—known as "jennies"—at the jackass's side while he was with the mare.

Washington's trick worked, and within a few years, there were mules all over Virginia and the Southern states, as Washington began selling Royal Gift's services to other farmers throughout the region. A few years later, Lafayette sent Washington another large jackass named Knight of Malta, who bred his own line for Washington and other farmers.[22] In short order, Washington had started a boom in American mule breeding. The creatures would provide invaluable services in the days before modern transportation and farm equipment. Even in the modern era, mules are often used when there is no other reliable form of transportation, such as in the large wilderness areas of California's Sierra Nevada Mountains.[23]

Breeding is one example of how Washington's private pursuits shaped our modern world. But his enterprises would also have an impact on the future of American agriculture, transportation, and manufacturing.

MOUNT VERNON'S COORDINATED ENTERPRISES

There are good entrepreneurs, great entrepreneurs, and a handful of extraordinary entrepreneurs. Washington became a great entrepreneur when he followed the in-

stinct that told him that oversupply, declining soil quality, and regulatory barriers signaled a dismal future for
tobacco, while increased demand combined with ease of
cultivation led to a bright future for wheat. Transforming
Mount Vernon from a tobacco plantation into a diversified farm with wheat as its main crop was a great entrepreneurial feat. But he went from a great entrepreneur to an
extraordinary one by building on his innovations with a
series of new, interconnected enterprises.

Seeing that there was such a large domestic and foreign market for wheat, Washington reasoned that his customers would also buy flour—instead of grinding their
own—if the price was right and the quality was assured.
But he needed a working mill—called a gristmill—to
make wheat into flour.

A gristmill had been on the property for more than
25 years, but it was in a state of utter disrepair. So in 1769,
Washington decided to build a new one. After consulting
with regional experts, Washington had his workers float
large river rocks from the falls of the Potomac River to
Mount Vernon lands at the riverbank and cut down timber on the Mount Vernon grounds, where he directed
them to build a mill that was three stories high.

Gristmills in those days were powered by a wooden
waterwheel. Standing about 40 feet high, the wheel had
numerous blades and a bucket to scoop up falling water
and harness its energy. But they usually needed to be very
close to a lake or river for a steady water supply. Washington's first problem was that the mill lacked a sufficient
supply of water for the wheel to function.

So Washington directed the building of a new mill

dam—according to Lengel, digging alongside his workers to construct an earthen canal called a millrace.[24] Then a wooden "water gate" was built to control the velocity of the water. The mill operator would open the gate somewhat or all the way depending on how much power he needed to grind the grain.[25]

Washington imported two large French buhrstones that, according to Lengel, were the best grinding stones "to be found anywhere, since they were exceptionally hard and held a good sharp edge for many years." Washington paid almost twice what he would have paid for local stones. Evidently he believed that the returns on the premium flour they would enable him to mill would more than recoup his investment.[26]

As with every new enterprise, there were setbacks. The water could freeze during the winter and the canal would flood during heavy rains. But overall, the gristmill was a smashing success. According to Lengel, by the end of the 1760s the productivity of Washington's flour-making operation had increased 25 times.[27]

Washington soon began milling the wheat and corn of neighboring farmers for a fee. At its peak, the mill ground 275,000 pounds of wheat into flour. Moreover, even before the Revolutionary War, Washington's flour was shipped all over the American colonies and exported as far as England and its colonies in the West Indies.[28]

Washington also pioneered in the distribution of branded food products by attaching the "G. Washington" imprint to all his bags of flour. "Washington" flour "became known for its reliable superiority," Lengel writes.[29]

In the early 1770s, he expanded the brand to the production of cornmeal and biscuits, which he also exported.[30]

Meanwhile, as a legislator in the House of Burgesses, Washington took the lead in creating an early form of trademarking that helped him and other Virginia flour-makers brand their products. As he described it in his diary entry of April 3, 1772—the day it was presented to the full House—there were two parts to the bill. One was "designed 'to prevent frauds, which may be committed by millers, bakers, and others, employed' in Virginia's growing flour export trade." This would be achieved by requiring that "All flour for export must be 'genuine and unmixed with any other grain, and . . . all of the same fineness, and faithfully packed in good casks, made of seasoned timber, and, when delivered, well and securely nailed.'"[31]

Many regulations today are rightly criticized as limiting consumer choice, protecting established firms by limiting competition, and escaping accountability through being issued by a remote bureaucracy. Washington's bill contained regulation, but it was limited to the core governmental function of protecting consumers from fraud. It did not restrict free entry into the flour-making business by placing limits on the number of manufacturers. And it came straight from the House of Burgesses, an elected body that could be defeated in the next election, making it far different from British edicts imposed on the colonists without their consent.

And the second part of the Burgesses' bill was a revolutionary step that anticipated the widespread trademarking of brands that has become an essential element of modern economies. The bill provided that once these measures to prevent impure flour from being exported were fulfilled, the manufacturer could register his brand with the county courts. Washington himself did just this a few months after the bill was passed. On December 21, 1772, Washington registered the "G. Washington" brand for his flour with the Fairfax County court in accordance with the new law he had helped draft.[32]

Unlike raw tobacco, Washington found that he was able to command a steady price for his flour, a processed foodstuff that he branded both with Mount Vernon's reputation for quality and with a trademark that had at least some legal protection. Up to this time, protecting a business firm's trademark had been a part of English common law, but this was one of the first instances in which trademark protection was written into the law of a specific jurisdiction.

It would be more than a century before the U.S. Congress passed its first trademark protection law. Although the first federal patent and copyright laws were passed in the 1790s and signed into law by President Washington, trademarks would go largely unprotected until the latter half of the next century.[33]

Some of the oldest trademarks in use today are those issued to Kellogg's cereals, Carnation condensed milk, and Heinz condiments.[34] Yet more than 100 years before Henry John Heinz began affixing the Heinz label to ketchup and horseradish to assure customers of their quality, Washington did roughly the same thing by registering and utilizing the "G. Washington" brand for his flour. Many business scholars, overlooking Washington's example, cite Heinz as the first businessman to brand food products. As business historian Richard Tedlow has written, "most manufacturers were unknown to the people who bought their products."[35] No evidence has emerged that Washington's example influenced Heinz or other food producers. But at the very least, he seems to be a prominent exception to the rule that most were unknown to their customers.

Washington plowed the profits from the gristmill into even more enterprises at Mount Vernon. As Ron Chernow writes, "Washington presided over a small industrial village at Mount Vernon." This village (as mentioned earlier) would come to include a fishery, a dairy, a textile and weaving factory, and a blacksmith shop.[36]

All these businesses were interrelated on some level. For instance, in a six-week fishing season each spring, using rowboats and large nets, Washington's men netted about 1.5 million fish—mostly herring, but also shad, bass, carp, perch, and sturgeon—from the Potomac River to be sold throughout the colonies and in the West Indies.[37] As described by the Mount Vernon Digital Encyclopedia, "the fish would be gutted and packed in salt, tightly layered in barrels, head to tail and upside-down so salt filled the interior cavities."[38] The inedible portions were used as fertilizer for crops such as wheat, which fueled the cycle of production at the gristmill.[39]

Washington's blacksmith shop provides another example of integration of Mount Vernon enterprises.

Smiths from the shop likely repaired iron equipment for the gristmill. Cleve irons from the shop may have been used to split grain in Mount Vernon's fields, and plows were made to furrow them. Iron horseshoes and nails were utilized in the care and handling of the horses that performed vital functions throughout the Mount Vernon estate. Those working at the shop included both journeymen craftsmen hired by Washington as well as some of Mount Vernon's enslaved population who were trained as blacksmiths. Accounts for the shop list a total of 134 customers outside of Mount Vernon for the period from 1755 to 1799, the year of Washington's death.[40]

Archaeologists and scholars now believe that there were several more items of particular interest that were made at the shop at various times from the 1750s onward. They were items that were always of necessity for colonial families, but that would take on additional purposes as hostilities with the British increased. These were triggers, breech plugs, and other parts needed to make and repair colonial guns.[41]

CHAPTER 8

SUCCESS AND REVOLUTION

*Martha Washington's Spinning House for Textile Making
as Reconstructed at Mount Vernon*

IT IS STILL NOT COMPLETELY UNDERSTOOD WHY MEMBERS of the Continental Congress—a contentious group of delegates hailing from all 13 colonies—were so confident in Washington that they unanimously made him general of the Continental Army on the first ballot in 1775. Several theories have been offered, including the fact that he wore his uniform from the French and Indian War to sessions of Congress, and that John Adams' vouching for him won over other members from the Northern colonies.[1]

Largely overlooked is the fact that Adams specifically cited Washington's business success in making the case for him to lead the American forces. Adams recorded in his diary that he declared to the Congress "that I had but one Gentleman in my Mind for that important command, and that was a Gentleman from Virginia who was among Us and very well known to all of Us, a Gentleman whose Skill and Experience as an Officer, whose independent fortune, great Talents and excellent universal Character, would command the Approbation of all America, and unite the cordial Exertions of all the Colonies better than any other Person in the Union: Mr. Washington."[2]

This endorsement didn't come out of nowhere. Nor was it a hard sell for Adams. Washington was already a figure of some renown in the colonies, and that renown was based—as Adams specified—not just on his exploits in the French and Indian War, or on his sterling character, but also on the "independent fortune" that he had built through his own hard work and business acumen.

For one thing, as a man of means, Washington would not be compromised by personal financial concerns while serving as general, a fact that he confirmed when he refused to take a salary (though he did request an expense account, which could be rather lavish at times).[3] But it was not illogical to think that running a successful business enterprise was a good prerequisite for commanding an army. An army is very like a business in some ways, and Washington's correspondence during the war gives ample proof of his constant concern for the food, supplies, personnel, and weapons that he needed to hold it together through so many ups and downs.

We also know that Washington's business successes and the fear that the British could take it all away was a strong factor that swayed him in favor of breaking away from Britain and creating an independent republic. Throughout the 1760s, Washington watched an increasingly interventionist British government frustrate the efforts of entrepreneurs like himself, and he became increasingly concerned that Britain's power to levy taxes and impose regulations on the colonists without their consent could effectively shut down his gristmill and other enterprises.

This was not a new concern for Washington. As we have seen, one of the factors that led him to cease farming tobacco was the costs associated with shipping the product to Great Britain and obtaining a fair price. "Mother England" also prohibited exports of the American colonies' products to lands outside the British Empire. So one of the main advantages of producing products like wheat and flour, for which a domestic market existed, was avoidance of these fees and duties on goods shipped to the home country.

As Washington expanded his enterprises, British trade barriers, taxes, and regulations began to harm him in other ways. For instance, the Mount Vernon fishery used imported salt to preserve the herring before it was shipped. Portuguese salt was considered to be the best in the world for this purpose because it did not break down when put in contact with wet fish. But at the behest of British merchants, Great Britain began placing heavy restrictions on the importation of salt. A shipper could only bring Portuguese salt into the colonies if his ship were delivering a cargo to Lisbon, and only then if the ship first went to England and paid a tariff before sailing on to the colonies. This meant that colonial fisheries like Washington's most often had to use inferior salt from Liverpool, which could be so corrosive that it destroyed the tasty fat part and hardened the lean part of meat and fish.[4]

In order to understand why British taxes ultimately led to rebellion by Washington and other leading figures in the colonies, we must look at the regulations on trade and commerce to which the American colonists had been subjected since the first English settlers landed in Jamestown in 1607. Mercantilism was the order of the day. Parliament's Navigation Act of 1651 gave Britain complete control of trade routes, and colonists could generally only export and import to and from the mother country.

As the first stages of the Industrial Revolution began in the late seventeenth and early eighteenth centuries, Mother England would mostly forbid her "children" in the colonies from taking part in the manufacturing boom. Instead, the colonies would grow crops like to-bacco or mine resources such as iron ore to send to Brit-ain. The mother country would then manufacture goods with these materials and ship them back to the colonies.

These mercantilist practices continued even when they seemed to defy logic and imposed unnecessary costs on both parties. Recall that a few decades earlier, the British government encouraged prospecting for iron in Mid-Atlantic colonies, and the mining and smelting of that iron. In his *Notes on the State of Virginia* written during the Revolutionary War, Thomas Jefferson describes eight major iron facilities built in colonial Virginia and ac-knowledges there were probably more that hadn't been officially documented. He writes:

> The mines of iron worked at present are Callaway's, Ross's, and Ballendine's, on the South side of James river; Old's on the North side, in Albemarle; Miller's in Augusta, and Zane's in Frederic. These two last are in the valley between the Blue ridge and North moun-tain. Callaway's, Ross's, Millar's, and Zane's, make about 150 tons of bar iron each, in the year. Ross's makes also about 1600 tons of pig iron annually; Bal-lendine's 1000; Callaway's, Millar's, and Zane's, about 600 each. Besides these, a forge of Mr. Hunter's, at Fredericksburgh, makes about 300 tons a year of bar iron, from pigs imported from Maryland; and Taylor's forge on Neapsco of Patowmac, works in the same way, but to what extent I am not informed. The indications of iron in other places are numerous, and dispersed through all the middle country. The toughness of the

cast iron of Ross's and Zane's furnaces is very remarkable. Pots and other utensils, cast thinner than usual, of this iron, may be safely thrown into, or out of the waggons in which they are transported. Salt-pans made of the same, and no longer wanted for that purpose, cannot be broken up, in order to be melted again, unless previously drilled in many parts. In the western country, we are told of iron mines between the Muskingum and Ohio; of others on Kentucky, between the Cumberland and Barren rivers, between Cumberland and Tannissee, on Reedy creek, near the Long island, and on Chesnut creek, a branch of the Great Kanhaway, near where it crosses the Carolina line.[5]

It would have made obvious sense to build factories near these iron mines and furnaces. That way, the colonists would have ready access to finished goods, instead of having to pay the direct and indirect costs of shipping raw iron to Britain only to have iron goods assembled there and then shipped back to the colonies. Parliament, however, pushed through the Iron Act of 1750, which banned colonial manufacture of nearly all finished goods containing iron—including useful tools like knives, sickles, horseshoes, and nails—or any combination of iron with carbon or other elements to make steel.

The Iron Act decreed: "From and after the 24th day of June 1750 no mill or other engine for slitting or rolling of iron, or any plating-forge to work with a tilt hammer, or any furnace for making steel, shall be erected or continued in any of his Majesty's colonies in America. And if any person or persons shall erect, or cause to be erected . . . any such mill, engine, forge, or furnace, every person or persons so offending, they shall for every such mill, engine, forge, or furnace, forfeit the sum of £200 of lawful money of Great Britain."[6] The act further deemed such mills and factories "a common nuisance" and declared that every British-appointed colonial governor was "authorized and required to cause such mill, engine, forge or furnace to be abated" or shut down.[7]

There were similar acts that banned or restricted manufacture of specific commodities in the colonies. The Hat Act of 1732 banned exports of hats from the colonies and limited the number of workers colonial hatmakers could employ.[8] The Wool Act (or Woolen Act) of 1699 forbade export of wool to England from the colonies (and also from Ireland) and restricted trading of wool within the colonies in order to give a boost to English wool manufacturers.[9]

Even if no law specifically forbade the manufacture of a product, entrepreneurs knew that their new mill or factory could be closed at the whim of British officials if domestic manufacture of the product made the colonies less of a captive market. As business and social historian Lyman Horace Weeks writes, "As soon as there were indications that manufacturing industries were like to develop in the colonies the jealousy of the British manufacturers was aroused, for they had always regarded America as an altogether exclusive market for their goods . . . The British government, acutely responsive to such argument, and also alive to the political importance of deriving revenue from the colonies and at the same time keeping them under control, discouraged and in every way endeavored to prevent the establishment of manufacturing enterprises that might be expected to adversely affect the interests of the mother country."[10]

For instance, when Philadelphia became the epicenter of American publishing, paper mills popped up all around Pennsylvania. Benjamin Franklin, whose printing business sold newspapers, books, and almanacs throughout the colonies, personally invested in 18 new paper mills.[11] Parliament took note of this development and issued a report in the 1730s warning that while American paper mills posed no threat of competition in Britain, their existence "certainly interferes with the Profit made by our *British* merchants" who traditionally supplied paper to the American colonists.[12]

One thing that mitigated these mercantilist statutes and regulations was the policy of "salutary neglect," whereby lax enforcement of these rules was condoned so long as colonial endeavors weren't seen as threatening general British prosperity. Rules weren't enforced uniformly across the colonies. Sometimes this was due to colonists bribing or granting favors to the appointed royal governors, who frequently used their offices to enrich themselves.

As a result, some paper and iron mills and other factories continued to be built, including the blacksmith shop that made horseshoes and nails at Mount Vernon. (Gristmills, like that at Mount Vernon, which processed crops into foodstuffs such as flour, were also generally exempt, though this could always change.) However, these enterprises were generally small scale, both because of limited resources and also by design, so as not to attract the notice of a particularly zealous British official.

All this changed in the early 1760s, when the British imposed new rules and taxes after the French and Indian War. At first, the new taxes and trade barriers erected by the British under King George III didn't affect Washington directly. But he bristled at their effects on his fellow colonists. Often, these taxes had their real bite in the oppressive regulations that came attached to them. The Stamp Act, for example, did more than just tax the colonies on the paper they used from Britain. That in itself might not have been so bad, as the colonists could simply build more paper mills to supply their growing needs. Yet it also mandated that virtually all printed material in the colonies—including legal documents, magazines, newspapers, pamphlets, and even playing cards—be produced with stamped paper from Britain. Further, the colonists would have to purchase the stamps themselves with British currency of gold and silver coins, which was scarce in the colonies. As historian Paul Johnson notes, whether by accident or design, "there was simply not enough cash available for most people to pay [for] the stamps."[13]

This tax/regulation scheme inspired immediate and widespread opposition. In addition to the cost burden, colonists hated the sheer complexity of figuring out the number of stamps needed in each case. The tax on pamphlets, for instance, increased per number of pages but decreased if the document was large enough to be deemed a book.[14]

These taxes were the proverbial "straw that broke the

camel's back" after decades of mercantilism that limited the colonists' economic opportunities. As Woody Holton writes in his pioneering economic analysis of the causes of the Revolution, "historians have focused on the straw and ignored the enormous burden the camel already carried."[15] The colonists' opposition to the new taxes "can seem selfish, or their fears of parliamentary tyranny can seem like paranoia, until it is remembered that they already paid a 'heavy tax' to Britain in the form of its costly monopoly of their trade."[16]

This burden was detailed in an impassioned letter to Franklin by a Philadelphia merchant whom historians believe to be Charles Thomson, an Irish immigrant who owned a dry goods store in Philadelphia and would later organize local citizens against British rule. Thomson would go on to serve as secretary of the Continental Congress, co-own a failed distillery and a successful iron factory, and become the first American to translate the Bible into English.[17] His letter, which Franklin arranged to be published anonymously for a British audience in the *London Chronicle* in 1765, argued that the Stamp Act was especially unjust given the sacrifices the colonists had already made.

Referencing the Iron Act, the Hat Act, and the Wool Act, Thomson wrote: "That the Colonies have borne a great deal before they complained, must be allowed, when we consider the several restrictions laid upon them. No one Colony can supply another with wool, or any woollen goods manufactured in it. The number of hatters must be restrained, so that they cannot work up the furs they take at their doors; nay a hat, though manufactured in England, cannot be sent for sale out of the Province, much less shipped to any foreign market. The iron we dig from our mountains, we have just the liberty to make into bars, but farther we must not go: we must neither slit it nor plate it, nor must we convert it to steel."[18]

It was especially unjust not to allow the colonists to make steel and ship it to the mother country, Thomson argued, given that Britain imported steel from Germany. He also bemoaned the devastating effects of the Stamp Act on Pennsylvania's paper mills, which were "nursed with care and brought to so great perfection in this province."[19]

The colonists responded with widespread boycotts of British goods. Due to opposition from both the colonists and the British merchants hurt by these boycotts, Parliament repealed the Stamp Act in 1766. Yet in the same session, the legislative body thumbed its nose at the colonists by passing the Declaratory Act, affirming the right of Britain to tax the colonists without their consent.

A year later, Britain passed the Revenue Act of 1767, which levied taxes on paper, paint, lead, glass, and tea imported into the colonies. Then it passed a series of ever more coercive measures—often referred to as the Townshend Acts—for collecting these taxes and punishing those who evaded them. These measures authorized "general" warrants that allowed British officers to conduct random searches of American homes without specifying what they were looking for, trials for tax evasion by British judges conducted without juries, and even suspension of the New York Assembly when colonists there refused to provide accommodation and housing to British officers.

Seeing how the mother country was trampling on what he and other colonists assumed to be their rights and privileges as British citizens, Washington increasingly perceived a threat to all he had built. Washington expressed his thoughts in a 1769 letter to his neighbor George Mason, a scholarly man who would later author the Virginia Declaration of Rights, which in turn greatly influenced both the Declaration of Independence and the Bill of Rights.

Washington's letter has been noted by many scholars as representing a turning point in how he viewed the colonies' relationship with Britain. James Thomas Flexner calls it "a major milestone of Washington's road to Revolution."[20] But the specific reasons Washington gives for turning against Britain have been largely overlooked. This is likely because these reasons can't really be grasped without an understanding of Washington's entrepreneurial activities up to this point.

In his letter, Washington expressed the fear that Britain would not just tax the goods he purchased but shut down his new enterprises through regulation. "I have always thought that by virtue of the same power (for here alone the authority derives) which assume's [sic] the right of Taxation, they may attempt at least to restrain our manufactories," Washington wrote. Speaking specifically of his gristmill and other manufacturing enterprises, Washington reasoned further that for Great Britain, it was "no greater hardship to forbid my manufacturing, than it is to order me to buy Goods of them loaded with Duties, for the express purpose of raising a revenue."[21]

Note the words "me" and "my" in that sentence.

Washington was speaking about threats to his own personal enterprises—business ventures that had only been startups a few years earlier. He was also expressing a perennial fear still faced by entrepreneurs today: that of overweening regulation by bureaucrats unaccountable to the electoral process.

Washington wasn't alone in fearing that Britain's next move would be to stamp out manufacturing altogether through ever more burdensome regulation, including the actual shutdown of mills and factories. John Dickinson, a landowner and attorney beginning his political career, expressed this sentiment in the late 1760s in "Letters from a Farmer in Pennsylvania," an influential series of essays that persuaded many colonists to take up arms for independence. (Dickinson ironically would refuse to sign the Declaration—favoring more negotiation with Britain—as a delegate to the Continental Congress in 1776. He nonetheless fought as an officer in the Pennsylvania militia and was a delegate at the Constitutional Convention in 1787.)

In "Letter 2" of his series, published in the *Pennsylvania Gazette* on December 10, 1767, Dickinson proclaimed, "GREAT BRITAIN has prohibited the manufacturing [of] iron and steel in these colonies, without any objection being made to her right of doing it." Then he predicted, "The like right she must have to prohibit any other manufacture among us."[22]

Dickinson cited William Pitt, a member of Parliament and former prime minister who sympathized with the colonies in opposing the new taxes, but nonetheless asserted that it was otherwise appropriate for Great Britain to assert vast, nearly unlimited powers over the colonies. "We may bind their trade, CONFINE THEIR MANUFACTURES, and exercise every power whatever," Dickinson quoted him as saying.[23]

Holton notes that Washington, Dickinson, and others were right to worry about encroaching British regulations on American manufacturing. In 1774, Parliament tried to expand the ban on colonial wool production to linen, and a bill was introduced to ban the export to the colonies of "utensils" used in "cotton and linen manufactures."[24]

The response of Washington and many others was to double down on the type of manufacturing that had been banned or discouraged by the British. With Martha's help, Washington ramped up Mount Vernon's textile production. According to Chadwick: "Martha Washington turned an outbuilding into a bustling clothing factory. As a child in New Kent County, she had been taught how to use spinning wheels and other machines to produce clothing, and had also become an expert sewer and a wizard at needlepoint; she had mastered the production of quilts. She, in turn, taught the domestics at Mount Vernon how to sew, and from time to time, hired local women to assist in the production of clothing."[25]

With textile production, George and Martha once again integrated Mount Vernon's various enterprises, including its crops and livestock, as hundreds of sheep roamed the grounds. As early as 1766, Washington would breed what he called "my English ram lamb" with 65 female ewes. By 1775, 403 sheep were shorn for their wool. The Washingtons would continue to grow their flock even after the winning of the war lessened the need for home-made textiles. In the summer of 1799, just a few months before his death, Washington recorded 640 sheep at Mount Vernon.[26]

Historian Mary Thompson notes that while breeding sheep was "a pretty new concept in the 18th century," Washington obsessed over the details of the care necessary to produce fine wool. He corresponded about his sheep with several British agricultural experts, such as Arthur Young, and boasted that he sent a sample of Mount Vernon wool to British manufacturers who "pronounced it to be equal in quality" to the prestigious wool from Kent, England.[27]

Cotton, wool, and flax that was woven into linen were some of the materials used in Mount Vernon's textile production, much of which was overseen by Martha. There was a small crop of cotton grown at Mount Vernon, and she also directed that cotton be sent from one of the plantations in the Custis estate, in which she retained a life interest. Martha also oversaw the workers in the textile shop, who were both enslaved and hired laborers. In 1766, the Washingtons hired expert weaver Thomas Davis, who had recently arrived in the colonies from England. Between 1767 and 1771, Martha asked Davis to make popular fabrics of the day, such as mixtures of cotton and wool and cotton embedded with the repetitive "bird's eye" pattern that is still popular today. Martha's account book included over 60 outside customers.[28]

Mount Vernon's textile facilities also produced fishnets, harnesses, carpets, and quilted bedspreads called counterpanes. Under Martha's supervision and Davis' direction, Mount Vernon also made a very popular item called "bed ticking," which were cotton or linen pillow and mattress covers tightly woven to prevent the feathers inside from piercing through the fabric. Because George and Martha liked the job Davis was doing so much, and presumably wanted to keep him happy at Mount Vernon, they paid for his mother and sister to come over from England, as recorded one of Washington's ledgers.[29]

Yet even as Washington maintained his business connections in England, he was taking steps toward independence. In July 1774, shortly after Virginia's royal governor shut down the House of Burgesses for issuing proclamations against the British government, Washington sat down at Mount Vernon with his neighbor George Mason and wrote what has come to be known as the "Fairfax Resolves." As described by British historian Flora Fraser, the document was "at once an embryo bill of rights and a clarion call for a congress of delegates from all the colonies."[30]

Addressed officially to the British government, but written with the intent of rousing the colonists in the fight for economic—if not yet political—independence from Great Britain, the document contained 24 "resolves." These were a mixture of complaints against the British government, proclamations of natural rights, and calls to defy British regulations on manufacturing.

The first "resolve" proclaims that Virginia "can not be considered as a conquered Country," and that its "present Inhabitants are the Descendants not of the Conquered, but of the Conquerors." The colonists who landed in Virginia "brought with them" full English liberties, and their descendants were "entitled to all it's [*sic*] Privileges, Immunities and Advantages; which have descended to us their Posterity, and ought of Right to be as fully enjoyed, as if we had still continued within the Realm of England."[31]

The Resolves point out that up to this time, Virginia had accepted British mercantilism, even as it deprived the colonists of the higher prices for exports and lower prices for imports that free trade could yield to them: "As it was thought just and reasonable that the People of Great Britain shou'd reap Advantages from these Colonies adequate to the Protection they afforded them, the British Parliament have claimed and exercised the Power of regulating our Trade and Commerce, so as to restrain our importing from foreign Countrys, such Articles as they cou'd furnish us with, of their own Growth or Manufacture, or exporting to foreign Countrys such Articles and Portions of our Produce, as Great Britain stood in Need of."

The colonies had "chearfully acquiesced" to these practices as long as they were "directed with Wisdom and Moderation." However, "the Claim lately assumed and exercised by the British Parliament" was that "of making all such Laws as they think fit, to govern the People of these Colonies, and to extort from us our Money with out our Consent." Not only are such abuses of power "diametrically contrary" to traditional English liberties, they are "totally incompatible with the Privileges of a free People, and the natural Rights of Mankind."

Washington and Mason called on their fellow Virginians to stop exporting and importing goods to and from

Great Britain as long as these abuses persisted. They further urged them to build more mills and factories, and to facilitate cooperation and trade with the other colonies. At the same time, just one year before Washington would be appointed head of the Continental Army and two years before the colonies would formally declare independence, Washington and Mason expressed "that it is our greatest Wish and Inclination, as well as Interest, to continue our Connection with, and Dependance upon the British Government." But while they would be happy to remain "subjects" of Great Britain, "we will use every Means which Heaven hath given us to prevent our becoming it's Slaves."

Of course, when the document uses the analogy of slavery, it reminds modern readers of the persistence of African slavery in Virginia and other colonies. Remarkably, however, the slave trade is addressed in unusually critical terms. In Resolve 17, Washington and Mason state, "Resolved that it is the Opinion of this Meeting, that during our present Difficulties and Distress, no Slaves ought to be imported into any of the British Colonies on this Continent; and we take this Opportunity of declaring our most earnest Wishes to see an entire Stop for ever put to such a wicked cruel and unnatural Trade." Washington's growing antipathy toward slavery would culminate in his freeing all his slaves some 25 years later.

The Resolves were presented the next day at a meeting of Fairfax County property owners, where they were enthusiastically approved and signed by 24 of the county's leading residents. The document was then presented in August to the delegates at the Virginia Convention, which replaced the sessions of the House of Burgesses that had been suspended, and after that it was presented to the Continental Congress in the fall of 1774. It likely influenced fellow Virginian Thomas Jefferson in drafting the Declaration of Independence, which used similar language about grievances against the British and the violations of natural rights.

Another publication in 1776 radically turned people against mercantilism in both the colonies and Great Britain. In his book *An Inquiry into the Nature and Causes of the Wealth of Nations*, Scottish economist and moral philosopher Adam Smith pointed out how restrictions on imports and exports were driving up prices for both America and Britain, as well as for import/export businesses in both countries.

Smith also argued that enlightened self-interest benefitted the economy as a whole. His famous argument that the "invisible hand" of the market produces fair and just outcomes without governmental interference had particular appeal for entrepreneurs in new industries, such as Washington. Scholars have already pointed out Smith's influence on founding fathers such as James Madison.[32] Thanks to Hayes, we know that Washington also owned and likely read this book—indeed, he wrote notes in the margins.

Washington would utilize the phrase most associated with Smith—the "invisible hand"—in one of the most important speeches in American history. Upon his inauguration on April 30, 1789, Washington proclaimed, "No People can be bound to acknowledge and adore the *invisible hand*, which conducts the Affairs of men, more than the People of the United States. Every step, by which they have advanced to the character of an independent nation, seems to have been distinguished by some token of providential agency."[33]

Smith was writing in the context of trade and wealth distribution, whereas Washington was speaking of the several decisions of individuals that led to the transformation of the 13 colonies into an independent nation, which he believed was guided by "providential agency." Yet some scholars have found that their conceptions of an "invisible hand" guiding human affairs are not that different. Both men believed that the best results are most often achieved by the individual decisions of several people uncoerced by a centralized political authority. In the address, Washington said Americans' "important revolution just accomplished in the system of their United Government" resulted because of "the voluntary consent of so many distinct communities." Similarly, Smith wrote that "in the great chess-board of human society, every single piece has a principle of motion of its own."[34]

Yet both argued that such individual human actions leading to a greater social good could indeed be coordinated by a higher power. Just as Washington spoke of a "providential agency" in the inaugural address, Smith expounded on a "Providence" that "neither forgot nor abandoned those who seemed to have been left out in the partition."[35]

Smith's writings, notes University of Illinois professor Samuel Fleischacker, reinforced the views of the founding fathers that enlightened self-interest could be harnessed to serve the greater good. They "found in Smith support for the view that people's economic occupations could foster or dissipate their private virtues," Fleischacker observes.[36] Certainly, Washington's virtues were fostered when his new businesses encountered crushing British red tape.

* * *

This understanding of Washington's entrepreneurial activity as one of his main motivations for joining the movement for independence hearkens back to the thesis by Charles A. Beard and other progressive historians that the founding fathers were simply fighting for their economic self-interest.[37] The heart of Beard's theory has been debunked by subsequent historians, particularly Forrest McDonald and Gordon Wood, who have shown that there was no correlation between the wealth of individuals and whether they supported the revolution.[38]

Nevertheless, it doesn't blemish Washington's character to say that he was fighting for his interest—and that of the other colonists—in being able to exercise his economic liberties free of arbitrary government interference. Moreover, Washington knew that he was putting much at risk in joining the independence movement.

As Lengel writes: "Military conflict threatened Washington's personal ruin as well as America's economic destruction. As he had learned during the French and Indian War, his prolonged absence from his estate was a recipe for its eventual degradation . . . It is a measure both of Washington's realism and of his belief in the cause that he accepted the risk not just to participate in the war but to lead the army."[39]

George would spend the next eight years on various battlefields, where Martha would frequently join him. But the businesses they ran at Mount Vernon were never far from their minds. They would both write detailed letters on operations to the managers of their various enterprises. On May 31, 1781, Martha penned a note from George's military quarters in the Hudson River Valley with questions and instructions for Mount Vernon farm manager Lund Washington. Referring to herself in the third person, she told Lund: "Mrs. Washington will be glad to know if the cotton for the counterpanes was wove and whitened. How many yards was there of it? How many counterpanes will it make?"[40]

The freedom to run Mount Vernon as they saw fit—and trade with whomever they wished—motivated both George and Martha to make this first of many sacrifices for themselves and their fellow Americans.

CHAPTER 9

FATHER OF INVENTION: WASHINGTON'S SUPPORT FOR EIGHTEENTH-CENTURY INNOVATORS

The Inside of Mount Vernon's 16-Sided Barn as Reconstructed from Washington's Design

As PRESIDENT, GEORGE WASHINGTON RECEIVED MANY RE-quests from ship captains or drivers of horses and carriages for permission to pass through secure areas without interference from the military or other authorities. Most of these requests were routine. However, on January 9, 1793, he granted a safe-passage request from the pilot of a highly unusual vehicle: a new invention called a hot-air balloon.[1]

Balloon flights had recently been pioneered by a small number of enthusiasts in Europe, drawing large crowds and causing a widespread sensation. French pilot Jean-Pierre Blanchard had successfully launched short flights in France and England and had also flown across the English Channel. Now he wished to bring his air show to America.

Not only did Washington allow it, he gave the visitor a hearty American welcome. Cannon fire, at regular intervals, awoke the capital city of Philadelphia on the same day Washington signed the letter of safe passage. At 10 a.m., in front of gathered crowds, Washington himself appeared to give Blanchard his pass and make a short speech praising the man he called "the bold aeronaut." Future presidents John Adams, Thomas Jefferson, James Madison, and James Monroe were also in attendance. After waving the flags of the United States and France to the crowd watching from the street and the windows of nearby buildings, Blanchard took off and covered 15 miles in a then unheard-of 46 minutes. He would return to Philadelphia by conventional travel later that evening to visit Washington and tell him all about the day's journey.[2]

Washington was already well aware of the phenomenon.[3] The craze had been kicked off ten years earlier, when the first manned balloon flight was launched in Paris by the Montgolfier brothers. The balloon was up in the air for a grand total of 25 minutes, and it traveled just about five miles. The public was fascinated, yet few grasped the implications for the future. Washington was one of those few.

Despite Thomas Jefferson's assertion that Washington's mind, though capable of making sound judgements, was "slow in operation, being little aided by invention or imagination," Washington was quicker than most of his contemporaries to see the potential of manned flight.[4] Writing to French military leader Louis Lebègue Duportail in 1784, Washington made this prediction: "The tales related of them are marvelous, and lead us to expect that our friends at Paris, in a little time, will come flying thro' the air, instead of ploughing the ocean to get to America."[5]

In fact, Washington saw the potential of many inventions of the early industrial age, and he gladly served as a mentor or booster for a number of other innovators. He championed inventors both in his policies as president and in his dealings with them as a private citizen.

Believe it or not, when the United States became a new nation in the 1780s, inventors didn't have the best public image. As Andrea Sutcliffe explains in her history of steam power, many people at that time viewed them as "self-indulgent crackpots."[6]

Fortunately, these individuals found an ally in Washington, who viewed them as visionaries desperately needed for the growth of the new nation. In his first address to Congress on January 8, 1790, Washington called for the "introductions of new and useful inventions from abroad" and "encouragement . . . of skill and genius in producing them at home."[7] Congress passed the Patent Act later that year for the purpose (in the Constitution's words) of "securing for limited times to authors and inventors the exclusive right to their respective writings and discoveries."[8]

In 1891, speaking at an event at Mount Vernon on the one hundredth anniversary of the Patent Act, Joseph M. Toner, an eminent physician and lecturer who had served as president of the American Medical Association and American Public Health Association, described Washington's crucial role in helping inventors. He told the audience that "the instances in which Washington gave encouragement to new inventions are numerous," and that Washington would always have "a kind word of encouragement for those working to the end of devising new methods and improved implements in any of the arts."[9] As Toner noted, Washington was likely sympathetic to their struggles because he had tried his hand at inventing a few labor-saving devices himself.[10]

In the 1780s, Washington made what he would call a "drill plow" or a "barrel plow" by putting wheels on a plow and attaching a barrel to it. The revolving barrel would carry the seeds he wanted to plant and drop them into small seeding tubes affixed under the plow. The tubes would then distribute the seeds in the field at precise angles. The improved spacing of the seeds led to better growth of Washington's crops. The plow also helped Washington pursue his longstanding goals of crop rotation and conservation. In what had been the cornfields, Washington's workers would put different types of seeds in each tube of the drill plow and plant corn, cabbage, potatoes, and peas all in one field with one device.[11]

Nevertheless, by 1797, Washington likely replaced his drill plows—which had limitations on rough terrain—with the new mechanized "threshing machines" he was buying to plow Mount Vernon's fields.[12]

Washington's penchant for mechanical tinkering combined with his knowledge of architecture led him to build unique structures around Mount Vernon to improve the efficiency of his farming. We have already discussed the "dung repository" he designed to preserve excess manure in its liquid form. During his presidency in the 1790s, Washington wrote letters to his Mount Vernon farm managers detailing the construction of a unique, 16-sided barn for grain storage and processing. The barn, completed in 1794 and reconstructed at Mount Vernon in 1996 from Washington's original plans, contained many unique, practical features. For instance, Washington deliberately left spaces between the floorboards to move the grain via ramps to the granary underneath while horses slowly paced the white oak floor. The design of the barn made the horses part of the grain refining process.

Yet it was a journey Washington took in 1784 to the western part of Virginia that would bring him into contact with an inventor who would change transportation, travel, and technology forever. Washington's purpose in traveling west—over 600 miles on horseback and by river ferries—was both to inspect some land he had acquired and to look for ways to shorten travel time through the formidable Allegheny Mountains. He worried that the new nation could come apart if transportation barriers impeded contact with lands west of the mountains.

In the days before modern transportation it was often easier to cross an ocean than to traverse a mountain range. Territorial disputes with foreign nations and Indian tribes was one reason. But there was also the sheer logistics of transportation through roadless, rough terrain.

Washington, now 52, had seen the area before in his travels as a surveyor and as a young soldier in the French and Indian War. As journalist and author Joel Achenbach writes in his book about Washington's visions for Westward expansion: "Of the men who would be known as the Founding Fathers, only Washington had routinely slept under the stars."[13]

Of course this time, Washington was traveling in a little more style. According to Achenbach, Washington and his companions—who at various points included his friend James Craik (a personal physician of Washington's who had also served with him in the French and Indian War), Craik's son William, and Washington's nephew Bushrod (who would become a future Supreme Court justice)—traveled with silver spoons and cups, Madeira wine from Portugal, tea, seven pounds of sugar, oil, vinegar, mustard, and two kegs of West Indian rum. Washington didn't drink rum, but as Achenbach points out, it was "ideal for trading with frontiersman or securing thirsty guides through the backwoods."[14] Three servants—who may or may not have been enslaved—and three horses traveled ahead with the rest of their baggage.[15]

But no matter how many luxuries Washington brought along, he couldn't escape the reality of the rough roads. As Achenbach writes: "Roads in America were often hardly more than trails, choked with stumps, particularly south of the Potomac . . . Travelers in this part of the world would be bewildered by roads that forked promiscuously, that refused to go in a straight line, that seemed utterly overmatched by the rugged topography along the Potomac and its tumbling tributaries. Throughout the United States, bridges over major rivers simply didn't exist."[16]

To the extent it was possible, improving navigation through rivers themselves seemed to be the best way to ease long-distance travel. Washington and others saw opportunities to make these improvements on the Potomac River, which spanned from Maryland's western shore at the Chesapeake Bay to the Fairfax Stone by the Allegheny Mountains in what is now West Virginia, passed by the city of Alexandria, and came literally to Mount Vernon's backyard. These entrepreneurs envisioned building a series of canals to make the Potomac more navigable. The next year, they would pool their investments into the Potomac Company—a firm with special charters from Maryland and Virginia—to pursue these aims.

Washington also sought out new types of seacraft that promised speedier and smoother travel on the river. When he arrived in Bath, Virginia (now Berkeley Springs, West Virginia), he thus became enthralled with a local inventor who was designing a new kind of boat.

James Rumsey, a 41-year-old builder and jack-of-all-trades, was part-owner of the inn in Bath where Washington was staying. In the little spare time that he had, Rumsey built a model of a "pole boat," which would propel itself upstream through the maneuvering of wooden poles. Many of the townspeople had treated the invention with scorn, but Washington let Rumsey make his case. Washington watched as the inventor placed his mini-vessel, roughly the size of a toy boat, into a stream that flowed into the Potomac. Washington was awed as the boat propelled itself against a rapid current.

Subsequently, Washington wrote a letter of endorsement to help Rumsey secure funding from investors and patent rights from state legislatures (there would not be a U.S. Patent Office until after the U.S. Constitution authorized one). Rumsey, wrote Washington, "has discovered the art of working boats by mechanism," and asserted that "this discovery is of vast importance."

As Sutcliffe writes, "Washington's influence was golden" when Rumsey approached the legislatures of Virginia and other states.[17] As then–Virginia state delegate James Madison would write to Thomas Jefferson in 1785, when Rumsey had visited the legislature just a year earlier, "the apparent extravagance of his pretensions brought a ridicule upon them, and nothing was done." But when the legislators learned of Washington's endorsement, "it opened the ears of the Assembly."[18] Rumsey was granted a patent by Virginia, as well as by Maryland and Pennsylvania.

Rumsey's original design of a "pole boat" would never sail as a full-sized vessel. And for some Washington biographers, the story ends there. They describe Rumsey as a failed inventor, and some suggest that he bamboozled Washington into writing his letter of endorsement.

Ron Chernow spends less than a paragraph describing how Washington supposedly "came under the sway of a gifted inventor endowed with glib patter." Hinting that Rumsey pulled the wool over Washington's eyes, Chernow writes that Washington was "beguiled" by Rumsey's "ungainly invention."[19] Edward Lengel describes Washington's relationship with Rumsey with similar sentiments: "Agog with visions that the boat could be 'turned to the greatest possible utility in inland Navigation,' Washington provided Rumsey with a certificate of approval."[20] Richard Brookhiser declares flatly that "Rumsey's boat never worked."[21]

With all due respect to these otherwise excellent biographers, their accounts of this episode are akin to describing Thomas Edison as a failed inventor due to his hundreds of unsuccessful attempts to create a light bulb, without mentioning that his final attempt was a success. In fact, Rumsey would build a working steamboat just three years after he and Washington met.

Many of the scientists aware of Rumsey's achievement have written in technical journals and not in the popular press. Meanwhile, the false narrative that Robert Fulton invented the steamboat has been asserted widely in history texts. Fulton did not "invent" the steamboat any more than Henry Ford invented the car. Both men modified an existing design and got backing to make it commercially successful.

As his experiments progressed, Rumsey decided to

use steam to power his boat—a radical notion at the time. Benjamin Franklin, one of America's leading scientific minds, was skeptical that steamboats would ever be a practical form of travel. According to Sutcliffe, Franklin thought that "steam was not a strong enough force to move boats upstream."[22]

But Washington kept an open mind. He arranged for Rumsey to be hired as superintendent of the Potomac Company as it was improving navigation on the river. Not only did Rumsey receive steady income, he got the opportunity to test boats in various parts of the Potomac.

When word got around of Rumsey's progress, competition to build a passenger steamboat was spurred. Pennsylvanian John Fitch was also able to gather support for the steam-powered vessel he was building. When Fitch visited Mount Vernon to ask Washington for an endorsement, he politely declined and warned Rumsey in a letter to speed up, as "many people guessing your plan have come very near the mark."[23]

On August 22, 1787, Fitch demonstrated his boat on the Delaware River before the delegates attending the Constitutional Convention in Philadelphia. He offered boat rides to the delegates, taking them a few hundred yards on the river and back. Not to be outdone, Rumsey debuted his own steamboat on December 3 of that year on the Potomac River in Shepherdstown, Virginia (now in West Virginia). Instead of offering the equivalent of carnival rides, as Fitch had done, Rumsey took several of the town's leading ladies (including Mrs. Rumsey) on a two-hour river voyage.

Though the boat traveled just six miles, the townsfolk

had never seen anything like it. No one had. As aerospace engineer and author Rand Simberg has written, the steamboat was "the first vehicle to be moved by something other than animals (including humans), or wind or current."[24] A shared patent for the steamboat was awarded to both Rumsey and Fitch by the newly formed U.S. Patent Office in 1791.

After his successful voyage, Rumsey traveled to London to discuss a potential business deal with inventor James Watt and his business partner, Matthew Boulton, that would merge Rumsey's working boat with Watt's superior steam engine. Unfortunately, negotiations broke down and Rumsey suffered a stroke shortly thereafter and died in London in 1792.

Fifteen years later, Robert Fulton, who had met with Rumsey in London, would strike a similar deal and place Watt's engine in a boat that was influenced by Rumsey's designs. Fulton also had assistance from his wife's uncle, Robert Livingston, a well-connected figure who had signed and helped draft the Declaration of Independence and later served as U.S. minister to France. With financial backing secured by Livingston, Fulton began sailing his steamboats on regular routes from New York City to Albany in 1807, and as far as St. Louis, Missouri, by 1811.

In his 1944 book, *Steamboats Come True: American Inventors in Action,* James Thomas Flexner makes clear that while Fulton, like Henry Ford, was an excellent entrepreneur who created a new industry, he added very little to Rumsey and Fitch's innovations. Fulton was "unoriginal and by no means as brilliant an inventor as some of his rivals," Flexner declares.[25] Similarly, Robert O. Woods, a fellow with the American Society of Mechanical Engineers, writes in 2009 that "the real innovators behind steam propulsion were John Fitch and James Rumsey."[26]

Fulton's commercial success led to him being falsely credited as the steamboat's inventor, despite the fact that Rumsey and others had secured a patent during Washington's presidency. Meanwhile, just as Rumsey and Washington had envisioned, the steamboat ultimately brought the country closer together. Steamboats shrunk travel time from point to point dramatically. When Fulton debuted his steamboat, called the Clermont, in 1807, it reduced sailing time from New York City to Albany—a 150-mile journey up the Hudson River—from around four days to just over a day. In a few years, more advanced steamboats would reduce travel time even further. Sailing time on the Mississippi and Ohio Rivers for the 1,500-mile voyage from New Orleans to Louisville dropped from 25 days in 1816 to less than 5 days in 1853.[27] Furthermore, subsequent inventors applied steam power to the nation's first trains, mills, and factories, bringing Americans even closer through transportation, communication, and the availability of mass-produced manufactured goods.

Moreover, the invention and successful commercial operation of the steamboat ushered in a turning point—a societal shift necessary for innovation to thrive. For the first time in history, the inventor became a cultural hero.

Economist Deirdre McCloskey writes that by the mid-nineteenth century in the United States and much of Europe, the inventor had become "an acknowledged benefactor of the world." This in turn started a virtuous cycle in which more talented people would chase glory and riches in their quest to invent the next big thing. According to McCloskey, "what mattered were two levels of ideas: the ideas for the betterments themselves (the electric motor, the airplane, the stock market), dreamed up in the heads of the new entrepreneurs drawn from the ranks of ordinary people; and the ideas in the society at large about such people and their betterments."[28]

McCloskey notes that the lionization of the inventor began in the United States before it spread to Great Britain and much of Europe. "The Americans, then the British, and then many other people for the first time on a large scale, such as the Swedes late in the nineteenth century, looked with favor on the market economy, and even on the creative destruction coming from its profitably alert innovations."[29]

So how did America break from history and show the world how to love inventors? It had a lot to do with both the policies and example set by George Washington, who championed inventors both as president and in his dealings with them as a private citizen.

CHAPTER 10

❖━◉━❖

NEVER AT REST:
WASHINGTON'S FINAL YEARS

The Rebuilt Mount Vernon Whiskey Distillery

WASHINGTON'S SERVICE AS GENERAL AND PRESIDENT EACH took him away from Mount Vernon for a period of roughly eight years. Upon each return, Washington would throw himself into growing the operations of the estate. Contrary to what some biographies, histories, and textbooks have stated, Washington was never "at rest" but remained active to the end of his life.

His return to Mount Vernon after two terms as president was a bit smoother than his homecoming after the Revolutionary War. During his presidency, he was able to visit Mount Vernon a few times and oversee operations. He was even able to make some major improvements during this time. For example, after personally signing the patent awarded to inventor Oliver Evans for an automation system for mills, Washington directed his estate managers to implement Evans' system at the Mount Vernon gristmill. Even without electricity, the mill was almost fully automated through a system of conveyor belts and bucket elevators. As described by *Farm Collector* magazine, "The product wasn't touched by human hands from the time the grain was dumped into the receiving hopper until the finished flour flowed into a bin ready for packing into barrels or bags."[1] The process is still in use today as one of Mount Vernon's attractions.

During his presidency, as previously discussed, Washington also sent letters detailing the construction of the 16-sided barn for grain storage and processing that was completed in 1794. Yet serving as president had, on balance, hurt rather than helped his businesses' profitability.

Conscious of his public image and not wanting to look like he was bullying people of lesser means, Washington had to think twice before taking legal action against a delinquent tenant or purchaser. Those in debt to Washington were quick to realize his predicament, and many took advantage of it.[2]

Meanwhile, the costs of maintaining Mount Vernon as an unofficial national shrine soared higher than ever. More and more Americans wanted to see the unique home of the father of their country, especially when they might catch a glimpse of the man himself.

When it came to visitors, Washington had an open-door policy, albeit subject to certain limits. "I have no objection to any sober or orderly person's gratifying their curiosity in viewing the buildings, Gardens, &ca. about Mount Vernon," Washington wrote to his farm manager William Pearce in 1794. However, he admonished Pearce not to give all visitors the *same* hospitality.

Washington's favorite Madeira wine from Portugal, for instance, should not "be given to every one who may incline to make a convenience of the house, in travelling; or who may be induced to visit it from motives of curiosity." It should only be given, Washington instructed, to the first couple's "*particular* and intimate acquaintance," "some of the *most* respectable foreigners," and "persons of some distinction (such as members of Congress &ca)."[3] For other visitors, Washington directed Pearce "to provide claret, or other wine on which the duty is not so high, than to use my Madeira."[4]

Washington also needed a new enterprise to solve a problem that had been vexing him for nearly 20 years. So he listened with an open mind when his recently hired farm manager James Anderson suggested building a distillery near his gristmill. The 42-year-old Scottish immigrant explained that it would be a natural fit with Mount Vernon's corn and wheat farming and processing operation and its easy access to water from the Potomac.

Anderson knew what he was talking about. For 19 years he had worked his own farm, mills, and distillery back in Scotland. But he lost almost everything in 1788 after several distilleries failed, and in 1790, he and his wife and seven children left Scotland and settled in Virginia.[5] There, he rented a farm where he grew crops and managed other peoples' plantations. He became farm manager at Mount Vernon in early 1797, just as Washington was coming home after serving as president.[6]

Since there weren't many books on distilleries, Washington relied on the expertise of others who had knowledge of both domestic and foreign whiskey markets. There were two regions of Great Britain known, then and now, for distilling high-quality spirits: Scotland and Ireland. Fortunately, Washington was able to turn for advice to his Irish-Catholic friend and former military aide, John Fitzgerald.

Fitzgerald had emigrated to the colonies in 1769, settling first in Philadelphia but moving to the port city of Alexandria near Mount Vernon. There he became a merchant of various items, and Washington was one of his customers. When the Revolution started, Fitzgerald volunteered his services and Washington appointed him aide-de-camp. Fitzgerald was with Washington during the harsh winter of 1777–78 at Valley Forge, handling Washington's personal correspondence and other important tasks. He remained at Washington's side through many of the war's fiercest battles.

After the war, Fitzgerald went back to being a merchant in Alexandria, but with a lot more prestige. Washington boosted his status further by inviting him to parties at Mount Vernon and making him a director of the Potomac Company, formed by Washington and others to improve navigation on the river. Fitzgerald became president of the company in the 1790s, and in 1793 Washington appointed him collector of customs for the Port of Alexandria.

In 1786, thanks probably in large part to his connections with Washington, Fitzgerald was elected mayor of Alexandria even though Catholics were a tiny minority and had been subject to official persecution until only a few years earlier. Colonial Virginia enacted a law in 1642 that barred Catholics from holding public office and outlawed many Catholic public worship services. Due to this ill treatment, only about 300 Catholics lived in Virginia when the Revolution began. But as with other religious minorities, Washington was faithful to his words to the Touro Synagogue in Rhode Island to give "to bigotry no sanction." Other Americans followed his lead in due course.

By the late 1790s, Fitzgerald had added a rum distillery to the many successful enterprises he owned. So Washington wrote to ask him if he thought there would also be a ready local and national market for distilled whiskey. Fitzgerald replied to Washington, "I cannot hesitate in my opinion that it might be carried on to great advantage on your estate."[7]

The distillery was built close to the gristmill so that excess corn and grains from the farms could be used for whiskey. It was about twice as large as those of neighboring farms and was comparable to the distilleries in Anderson's native Scotland. According to researchers at Mount Vernon, Washington's distillery "measured 75 x 30 feet (2,250 square feet) while the average distillery was about 20 x 40 feet (800 square feet)."[8] It had five big copper-pot stills that held 616 gallons of whiskey and 50 mash tubs—each one a 120-gallon barrel made of oak—for mashing and cooking the grain. In Washington's day, fermenting the mash and cooking the grain all happened in the same tub.[9] The leftover grain slop was fed to Mount Vernon's 150 hogs.[10] Julian Ursyn Niemcewicz, a Polish writer and statesman who visited Mount Vernon in 1798, recalled that the distillery produced "the most delicate and the most succulent feed for pigs . . . [They] are so excessively bulky that they can hardly drag their big bellies on the ground."[11]

Washington's original recipe consisted of 60 percent rye, 35 percent corn, and 5 percent malted barley. This is the recipe utilized now at the rebuilt Mount Vernon distillery, which makes and sells its own whiskey. Washington's distillery also made whiskey flavored with cinnamon or persimmons. In addition, it produced apple, peach, and persimmon brandy, as well as vinegar.[12] Much of the whiskey was purchased by Alexandria merchants, who resold it in their shops.[13]

The distillery almost instantly became Mount Vernon's most profitable enterprise. In 1799, the last year of

Washington's life, it produced 11,000 gallons of whiskey and was one of the largest distilleries in the nation.

Finally, with Mount Vernon seemingly on firm financial footing, Washington turned to a project that he had long contemplated but had kept secret even from those closest to him: freeing his slaves and assisting them in their freedom.

* * *

It is quite true that a significant portion of Mount Vernon's workers were slaves. In the distillery alone, Washington assigned six slaves that we know of—Hanson, Peter, Nat, Daniel, James, and Timothy—to assist with liquor production under Anderson's supervision.[14] Today, Mount Vernon honors these men as "distillers" in the rebuilt distillery.

As Lengel writes, "Despite all of Washington's talents as an entrepreneur, enslaved men, women, and children had by their labor played a vital role in creating his wealth."[15] This is an aspect of Washington's legacy that deserves further consideration. For modern sensibilities, Washington's slaveholding is a permanent stain on his moral character. Our purpose is not to excuse Washington's ownership of slaves but rather to point out what is remarkable about him, namely his gradual recognition that it was an evil that should be abolished.

As his life progressed, Washington would increasingly recognize the evils of slavery. Washington scholar Fritz Hirschfeld argues that by the 1790s, Washington had become a "lukewarm abolitionist."[16] Similarly, historian

Henry Wiencek writes: "For his entire life he had been conditioned to be indifferent to the aspirations and humanity of African-Americans. Something happened to change and to set him radically apart from his peers and his family."[17]

Slavery in Virginia had existed long before Washington was born, and for the first decades of his life, he saw no need to question it. As he was building Mount Vernon, he acquired slaves just like other Southern plantation owners. But as he gradually moved Mount Vernon away from a traditional tobacco plantation to a multi-use farm and factory complex, he began to question and then develop an aversion to the institution. He was also affected by seeing blacks, free and enslaved, fight bravely on the battlefields of the Revolutionary War.

It was during the war that Washington took his first step toward mitigating the damages of slavery. By 1778, Washington had stopped selling his slaves, because he didn't want to break up their families. In a letter to his cousin Lund Washington, who was managing operations at Mount Vernon in his absence, George instructed Lund to never again sell any slaves without their consent, which none apparently ever gave. Wiencek observes: "Having witnessed the breakup of families in the past, Washington vowed never again to do such a thing himself."[18]

Washington's adamant refusal to sell his slaves would impose substantial costs as the slave population at Mount Vernon both aged and reproduced. As he moved away from labor-intensive tobacco farming, Washington began training his slaves for other tasks. But there was still a surplus of slaves from the tobacco days, and as Brookhiser notes, Washington would bear the expenses of feeding and clothing many slaves who "brought in little or nothing."[19] By the 1790s, about 42 percent of the more than 300 slaves at Mount Vernon were either too old or too young to work.[20] Yet Washington remained firm, writing to a friend in 1794, "I am principled against selling negroes, as you would do cattle at a market."[21]

Washington didn't have the benefit of later scholarship that showed the devastating impact the breakup of slaves' families would have over the generations, but he could easily see that it had a harmful effect. "To disperse the families, I have an aversion," Washington wrote in a 1799 letter a few months before his death.[22]

Ironically, the objective of keeping families together posed a vexing obstacle to plans he would develop to emancipate his slaves. While in 1799 Mount Vernon had 317 slaves, only 124 belonged to George. The rest belonged to Martha in a type of legal trust, or "dower," for her grandchildren, as they were the descendants of the slaves bequeathed by Martha's wealthy first husband, Daniel Custis.[23] Over the decades, many of the slaves from these two groups had married and created families. Yet under Virginia law, neither George nor Martha could free the slaves held in trust through the dower. This could only be done by Martha and Daniel Custis' descendants who would inherit the slaves.

Yet Washington was steadfast in his determination that his slaves would get both their freedom and a system of support. As early as 1786, he stated that slavery should be gradually abolished.

That year, John Mercer, who served as a captain

during the Revolutionary War and would be a Maryland delegate to the Constitutional Convention, asked Washington if he would accept one of Mercer's slaves as a loan repayment. Washington politely but firmly declined. "I never mean (unless some particular circumstances should compel me to it) to possess another slave by purchase," wrote Washington to Mercer. "It being among my first wishes to see some plan adopted by which slavery in this Country may be abolished by slow, sure, & imperceptable [*sic*] degrees."[24]

Aside from an anti-slavery paragraph of the "Fairfax Resolves," which Washington co-wrote with George Mason in 1774, this is Washington's first known statement of abolitionist sentiment. It would be far from his last.

Watching blacks do different jobs, and do them well— from the soldiers who fought on the battlefields to the slaves who showed they could adapt to new roles in the distillery and gristmill—led Washington to rethink what he had been taught all his life about their inferiority. He may never have come around to believing the races were fully equal, but he saw that slavery was holding blacks back from their full potential. In a 1792 letter to British agriculturalist Arthur Young, Washington wrote that "blacks are capable of much labour," but those who were enslaved had "no ambition to establish a good name." Washington prefaced this statement by saying that he was "speaking generally."[25]

Robert Dalzell, Jr., and Lee Baldwin Dalzell, respectively professor emeritus of American culture and former head of the library reference department at Williams College, argue that this letter represented Washington's "ma-ture sense of slavery's greatest single flaw as a system of labor." They write that Washington saw that "slaves had no opportunity to win respect or earn good reputations," and that the question of what they might "accomplish as free men . . . seemed implicit in Washington's line of reasoning." They conclude by observing that Washington's question was "remarkably free of the usual racist assumptions of his society."[26]

Washington would keep asking these questions for the next several years of his life—discussing them with friends who publicly opposed slavery such as the Frenchman Lafayette[27]—and he seemed to come up with some answers. In the summer of 1799, Washington drew up a new will. When he died suddenly in December of that year after riding his horse during a snowstorm, friends and even some family members were stunned at one of his bequests.

After providing that all his debts "be punctually and speedily paid" and ensuring the right and title to his estate to "my dearly beloved wife Martha Washington," Washington penned a three-page "Emancipation Clause," as it has been called. "Upon the decease of my wife, it is my Will & desire that all the Slaves which I hold in my *own right*, shall receive their freedom."[28]

Washington's will gave immediate freedom to Billy Lee, the slave who had worked as Washington's personal attendant—a job that was often "valet" and was performed by enslaved and free people—at Mount Vernon, on the battlefield of the Revolutionary War, and during Washington's presidency. Washington's will also created an annuity that would pay Lee $30 a year and (if Lee chose) free room and board at Mount Vernon for the rest of his life. "This I give him as a testimony of my sense of his attachment to me, and for his faithful services during the Revolutionary War," Washington stated.[29]

The will also provided support for many of his other former slaves. Washington stipulated that those "unable to support themselves" due to advanced age or disability be "comfortably cloathed & fed by my heirs."[30] These included his grandchildren, nephews, and nieces, who each got a part of Mount Vernon, which had grown to 8,000 acres.

Finally, the will provided for the education of many of the former slave children. For Wiencek, this provision shows that Washington was far ahead of his time in believing that blacks were not "inherently inferior" and that "with education and the opportunity to find work they could prosper as a free people." Wiencek explains, "Education for slaves—the very thought of it was revolutionary. With this clause, Washington overturned generations of prejudice."[31]

Wiencek argues that "the unique forcefulness of the language" Washington employed in the Emancipation Clause demonstrates Washington's sense of urgency on freeing his slaves and equipping them to pursue a better life. In other parts of the will, Wiencek notes, Washington used stock phrases like "I give and bequeath" and "I recommend." But when it came to freeing the slaves, he began to give orders. Washington wrote, for example: "I do hereby expressly forbid the sale . . . of any slave I may die possessed of, under any pretense whatsoever." Wiencek observes, "The Emancipation Clause rings with the voice of command; it has the iron firmness of a field order."[32]

And just in case anyone questioned that order, or any other in his will, Washington inserted into the document a binding clause that forbade legal challenges to his bequests and set forth procedures to resolve disputes outside the courtroom. Thus the will provided for arbitration by "three impartial and intelligent men"—one chosen by each of the disputing parties and the third chosen by the first two—whose decisions would be "as binding on the Parties as if it had been given in the Supreme Court of the United States."[33]

One year later, Martha followed George's wishes and freed his remaining 123 slaves. She also let them stay on at Mount Vernon if they had relatives among the dower slaves. Although research tracking the lives of the enslaved population at Mount Vernon is ongoing, it does appear that at least some of the slaves freed by Washington were able to purchase freedom for dower slaves from Martha's descendants. Washington's estate did indeed follow his command to support the elderly and disabled former slaves and paid out pensions to them until 1833, presumably when the last of them passed away.[34]

Washington was not perfect. Although he was the only founding father to free all of the slaves he held, he can certainly be faulted for not liberating them earlier or speaking out publicly—save for the Fairfax Resolves—against the evils of slavery.

That said, Washington's freeing of his slaves in his will was a powerful message in its time. Such an unusual act for any large slaveholder—let alone one as prominent as Washington—would not go unnoticed. Washington's posthumous gesture inspired the opponents of slavery and constrained its defenders' ability to utilize him in justification of their cause. Chernow concludes that Washington's act was an important gesture that "brought the American experience that much closer to the ideals of the American Revolution."[35]

CHAPTER 11

MOUNT VERNON AND WASHINGTON'S LEGACY

The Mount Vernon Mansion House
Welcomes Visitors Today

Photo by Kristen H. Murray

THE STORY OF MOUNT VERNON POST-WASHINGTON IS A story of entrepreneurship and initiative in itself.

The modern management of Mount Vernon began in the latter half of the nineteenth century. Washington's heirs had struggled to keep up the estate both as a working farm and a showplace for visitors, many of whom would show up unexpectedly.

In 1853, South Carolina native Louisa Cunningham was a passenger on a steamboat on the Potomac River and was shocked by Mount Vernon's decrepit appearance as the vessel passed it by. She wrote to her daughter, Ann Pamela Cunningham, "I was painfully distressed at the ruin and desolation of the home of Washington and the thought passed through my mind: Why was it that the women of his country did not try to keep it in repair, if the men could not do it?"[1]

The younger Cunningham took up her mother's suggestion and formed the Mount Vernon Ladies' Association (MVLA). After convincing Washington's great-grandnephew John Augustine Washington III to sell the association 200 acres of Mount Vernon land, including the "mansion house" where George and Martha lived, and the family tomb, the MVLA raised money from across the country to meet the asking price of $200,000. In 1863, the MVLA made the final payment and has been running Mount Vernon ever since.[2] The modern Mount Vernon, about 15 miles south of Washington, DC, now holds 500 acres of the original estate. Most of the other 7,500 acres have been subdivided into residential lots and are now dotted with suburban homes.

Since its founding, the MVLA has taken no government grants, relying exclusively on support from individuals, private foundations, and corporations. Through the decades, some of America's greatest entrepreneurs and innovators, feeling a kinship with Washington, have visited Mount Vernon and patronized it with special gifts. After visiting Mount Vernon with his wife, Henry Ford worried that part or all of the estate would be destroyed by fire. So he built and donated a special fire engine for the Mount Vernon grounds in 1923. He would provide more vehicles to the curators of Mount Vernon over the years, and his company continues Ford's philanthropy by donating cars and trucks to Mount Vernon to this day. Though Thomas Edison didn't donate the electrification services his firm provided to Mount Vernon, he did pay a visit in 1916 to personally inspect the electrical system that the estate had contracted with his firm to install.[3]

Over the past decade, MVLA's partnerships with foundations and corporations have added some new attractions to Mount Vernon that greatly enhance our understanding of Washington. The Donald W. Reynolds Museum and Education Center, opened on the grounds of Mount Vernon in 2006, has a display on the Mount Vernon fishery and other facets of Washington's career as a "visionary entrepreneur." Erected with a large grant from the foundation of the late Reynolds, a media magnate who owned the *Las Vegas Review-Journal* and several TV stations, the museum continues to utilize technology to better explain history. One of its latest attractions is a theater featuring a 4-D interactive video called "Be Washington" that reenacts situations Washington faced on the battlefield and during his presidency and allows viewers to choose different paths to resolve the situation. The viewers can then compare their decisions to those of Washington.

2006 also saw the opening of a rebuilt whiskey distillery thanks to a generous grant and the continued support from the Distilled Spirits Council of the United States and its member distillers. Visitors can see whiskey being made as it was in Washington's day and even buy a bottle in the gift shop.

Mount Vernon also features some of the animals that were on George Washington's farms, such as mules and sheep, and a camel every December to commemorate the one Washington once ordered to entertain guests. Limited farming of wheat and processing of flour take place, and the food is sent to the Mount Vernon Inn Restaurant. That restaurant features dishes from Washington's day as well as some modern fare. And unlike in Washington's day, all guests can be served Madeira wine—if they pay for it.

The modern Mount Vernon is also indispensable to those interested in researching George Washington's life—from elementary and high school students writing reports to scholars writing academic papers and books. In 2013, the Fred W. Smith National Library for the Study of George Washington was built on the Mount Vernon grounds. It is a 45,000-square-foot facility that holds the many books owned by Washington, as well as many ad-

ditional eighteenth-century books and important documents from the eighteenth and nineteenth centuries.

The Mount Vernon Digital Encyclopedia contains
entries on topics of various aspects of Washington's life
written by various scholars who donate their time. Mount
Vernon CEO Doug Bradburn, who first came to the estate as founding director of the library, says the goal of
the Digital Encyclopedia is to get reliable information
about Washington to show up in any conceivable Inter-
net query. The Digital Encyclopedia has had eight million
visits and is regularly cited in news stories.[4]

For more general info, MountVernon.org, the website
run by the modern Mount Vernon, has a search engine
with access to in-house articles on thousands of topics
related to Washington. If you're interested, for instance,
in what Washington would eat for breakfast, you'd find
that the breakfast dishes served at Mount Vernon included ham, cold corned beef, cold mutton, and red
herring, all garnished with parsley and vegetables from
Mount Vernon's garden. Chocolate was also a favorite
in beverages.[5] Many recipes for these dishes—adapted
to modern times and ingredients—can also be found on
the site.

Under "entrepreneur," numerous entries on the
gristmill, distillery, fishery, and many of Washington's
businesses appear. And if you type in concepts related to
business and politics to grasp Washington's insights on the
topic, many interesting entries come up. Type in "debt,"
for instance, and you'll get his actions and views on public debt—"Cherish public credit. One method of preserving it is to use it as sparingly as possible," Washington

declared in his Farewell Address—and info on his experiences as an entrepreneur getting into and out of debt.[6]

But the best way to glean knowledge from George Washington is to step into his shoes and see things from his perspective. And there are opportunities at Mount Vernon and elsewhere to do just that.

✳ ✳ ✳

As an innovator, scientist, and entrepreneur, there are many things George Washington would like and even marvel at in today's America. Recall Washington's amazement at the launch of hot-air balloons, writing to a friend that "in a little time," Americans and Europeans "will come flying thro' the air, instead of ploughing the ocean." How he would love the airplanes that made his prediction come true! And someone who ordered pineapple shipped from the Caribbean and built a greenhouse to grow oranges and lemons would be thrilled that his fellow countrymen could buy them at a local store or even order them instantly from home on a smartphone. Someone who was doing everything to make farming more efficient—from building better plows to introducing mules to America—would delight in learning that the natural gas that fueled the "burning spring" on his land in western Virginia and the small fires on the Millstone River in New Jersey was now fueling farm equipment and other powerful machinery. And a fellow who kept detailed ledgers and used invisible ink would be fascinated by the encrypted ledgers at the core of cryptocurrency and its associated blockchain technology, both of which promise new levels of privacy and efficiency in transactions.[7]

Washington would take a particular interest in how far technology has advanced in his first profession of surveying, as well as in the many ways it has remained the same. He'd also find it remarkable, but perhaps—in his mind—predictable, that two of his successors honored with him on Mount Rushmore also practiced this profession. In fact, all four presidents whose faces are carved into the rock worked in land surveying in some capacity.

Thomas Jefferson and Abraham Lincoln were both professional surveyors. Jefferson followed in the footsteps of his father, Peter, who was a surveyor and cartographer for most of his adult life. Some of Peter Jefferson's accomplishments include extending the boundary line between the colonies of Virginia and North Carolina in 1749 and helping to produce the first accurate map of Virginia in 1751.[8]

In 1773, Thomas Jefferson became surveyor of Albemarle County, which includes Charlottesville and Jefferson's home, Monticello. He would resign this post a year later but, like Washington, continue to conduct private surveys on his lands for the rest of his life. At the age of 66, Jefferson ran measuring chains through the woods at the edges of Monticello in an attempt to teach his grandsons the basics of surveying.

And in 1803, as president, Jefferson utilized the knowledge gained from surveying to negotiate the acquisition of western land from France in the Louisiana Purchase. The next year, Jefferson would appoint an experienced surveyor and cartographer named William Clark to accompany his personal secretary, Meriwether Lewis, to explore and mark the boundaries of these western lands.

Lincoln entered the profession of surveying in 1833, after the failure of his general store left him starved for cash. He became an assistant to the surveyor of Sangamon County, Illinois. Learning on the job and from books about surveying, Lincoln surveyed sites for roads, schools, and farmland. According to biographer Carl Sandburg, Lincoln's "surveys became known for care and accuracy and he was called on to settle boundary disputes."[9]

Lincoln would leave the county surveyor's office in 1836, but as with Washington and Jefferson, he benefitted from his surveying experience in his other careers. Illinois educator Tallia Del Bianco, who writes study guides on Lincoln, argues that Lincoln's surveying experience helped him greatly as a lawyer representing parties in land disputes. He also utilized his knowledge from surveying in his successful push for the Homestead Act of 1862, which laid out steps for settlers to occupy and then own parcels of federal land.[10]

Theodore Roosevelt never worked in surveying in a professional capacity, but he did complete at least one significant land survey. In 1913, four years after he left the White House, Roosevelt led an expedition into the Amazon jungle in Brazil to look for the River of Doubt, the very existence of which was in question. Roosevelt and his team found the river, and the former president drew a map of nearly 2,000 miles.[11]

Surveying today is a fascinating mix of the old and the new, blending tradition with modern technology. Many of the principles of surveying are the same as in Washington's day, and some of the equipment is, too. A tripod is still placed firmly on the ground. Yet the device atop that stick is not a simple compass. Instead it's often a computer and/or automated camera using GPS, lasers, and 3-D technology to measure boundaries and track soil quality and other physical conditions. Surveying is still relatively open to everyone, even those not pursuing a four-year college education. According to the federal Bureau of Labor Statistics, all that is normally required for most jobs as surveying technicians—those who assist surveyors by setting up the surveying equipment on a given piece of land—is a high school diploma.[12]

Actual surveyors, those who are responsible for interpreting the data captured by the surveying equipment and preparing reports, need additional education to obtain a state license. But states vary as to the level of education they require. Some mandate four-year degrees, but others still allow surveyors to get their license after an apprenticeship with a licensed surveyor.[13] George Washington's Virginia is one of those states that still holds to the apprenticeship tradition and does not require a degree.[14]

Washington was able to try his hand and advance rapidly in many fields, such as surveying and real estate, because there was relatively free entry into those professions. Today, there are restrictive licensing laws for almost every trade. This trend threatens equality of opportunity, social mobility, and the founding fathers' ideal of the "pursuit of happiness."

As Tyler Cowen, professor of economics at George Mason University and an expert on social mobility and innovation, writes in *Time*: "While once only doctors and medical professionals required licenses to practice, now it is barbers, interior decorators, electricians, and yoga trainers. More and more of these licensing restrictions are added on, but few are ever taken away, in part because the already licensed established professionals lobby for the continuation of the restrictions. In such a world, it is harder to move into a new state and, without preparation and a good deal of investment, set up a new business in a licensed area."[15]

The good news is that in recent years, many conservatives and liberals have begun pushing back against excessive licensing requirements that harm low-wage workers and small entrepreneurs. The Obama administration issued a 2015 report calling for states to dramatically roll back licensing requirements, and the Trump administration is continuing this crusade. Liberal groups like the Brookings Institution have made common cause with longtime licensing reform advocates like the libertarian Institute for Justice and my own group, the Competitive Enterprise Institute, in calling for an end to licensing that shields industry incumbents from competition rather than protects health and safety.[16]

One of Washington's reasons for contemplating rebellion was the increasingly arbitrary taxes and edicts from the British that he felt threatened his growing enterprises at Mount Vernon. Recall that he wrote to George Mason in 1769 that he worried that for Great Britain, it was "no greater hardship to forbid my manufacturing, than it is to order me to buy Goods of them loaded with Duties."

Today, arbitrary regulation poses a greater danger than arbitrary taxation. Or as my colleague Wayne Crews puts it, we face "regulation without representation" through the growth of the administrative state.[17]

Today, taxation may be excessive, but for the most part it is not without representation. If Congress legislates a 35 percent tax rate, the Internal Revenue Service does not attempt to collect taxes at a 40 percent rate. You can argue that the IRS can be too aggressive in collecting taxes, but the amount it collects is not in excess of what the law requires.

In contrast, federal regulators often make the law up as they go along, as their rules bear little or no relation to the laws Congress has written. These arbitrary rules have crippled farms, factories, and other businesses and have even sent some entrepreneurs to prison. A *New York Times* story recently chronicled the travails of family-owned Indian Ladder Farms, a fifth-generation farm operation near Albany, New York, describing how for weeks at a time, the small office staff must turn its focus "away from making money to placating a government regulator." Using data provided by the Mercatus Center at George Mason University, the *Times* found 5,000 federal rules and restrictions that apply to apple orchards like the one at Indian Ladder Farms. The farm owner said that these rules stem from at least four different agencies of the federal government.[18]

George Washington would be dismayed not only at the volume of this red tape, but at the division of government from which the bulk of it originates. The founders vested "all legislative powers" in Congress in Article 1, Section 1 of the Constitution. They set up the executive branch, overseen by the president, to enforce the laws written by Congress, the elected representative chambers of the American people and the sovereign states.

But "administrative law" upsets this carefully drawn separation of powers. Agencies use the thinnest of pretexts in statutes from Congress to make their own arbitrary rules. The EPA, for instance, has interpreted the term "navigable waterways" in the Clean Water Act to mean "wetlands" the size of a mud puddle. Washington, who cleared many a swamp at Mount Vernon, would have been stifled by this edict. In recent years, small farmers have gone to jail for clearing puddles and ditches the EPA later declared to be "navigable waterways."[19]

Or take the Securities and Exchange Commission (SEC), created by Congress in 1934 to regulate "securities," a term widely understood to encompass financial instruments like stocks and bonds. The SEC has stretched the term to claim jurisdiction over a variety of objects. In the 1940s, the Supreme Court upheld the SEC's deeming subdivisions of a Florida citrus grove as "securities."[20] The SEC has recently cited that precedent to claim jurisdiction over cryptocurrencies such as Bitcoin, despite a lack of authorization from Congress. New technologies do sometimes require policy changes, but these changes should come from Congress debating the issues and changing the laws if necessary, as Washington and the other framers intended, not from an edict by unelected bureaucrats.[21]

Washington warned against this type of encroachment by the executive branch on the people's representatives in a largely overlooked section of his 1796 Farewell Address. Washington called for "caution in those entrusted with its administration to confine themselves within their respective constitutional spheres, avoiding in the exercise of the powers of one department to encroach upon another." He then warned, "The spirit of encroachment tends to consolidate the powers of all the departments in one and thus to create, whatever the form of government, a real despotism."[22]

Fortunately, there are proposals to rein in the administrative regulatory state, such as the Regulations from the Executive in Need of Scrutiny (REINS) Act, which would require Congress to affirmatively approve the costliest regulations.[23] And after decades of deference to regulatory agencies in their interpretation of the laws, courts are finally starting to show some "judicial fortitude"—in the phrasing of American Enterprise Institute senior fellow Peter Wallison, who was White House counsel under President Ronald Reagan. Wallison points to renewed efforts by the courts to look at whether agencies are acting without Congress' assent.[24]

Washington foresaw a day when some parts of the Constitution might need to be changed. But he warned in his Farewell Address that this change must come through the amendment process laid out by the Constitution and not through usurpation.

"If in the opinion of the people the distribution or modification of the constitutional powers be in any particular wrong, let it be corrected by an amendment in the way which the Constitution designates. But let there be no change by usurpation; for though this, in one instance, may be the instrument of good, it is the customary weapon by which free governments are destroyed."

But along with these warnings, Washington sounded a positive note, observing that the United States is linked by a yearning for liberty and free commerce. "You have in a common cause fought and triumphed together. The independence and liberty you possess are the work of joint councils and joint efforts—of common dangers, sufferings, and successes."

Washington closed his address by announcing that as for himself, it was back to the business of business, backed by a government based on free commerce and the rule of law. "I promise myself to realize, without alloy, the sweet enjoyment of partaking, in the midst of my fellow-citizens, the benign influence of good laws under a free government, the ever-favorite object of my heart, and the happy reward, as I trust, of our mutual cares, labors, and dangers." This "happy reward" is what every concerned citizen should strive for in preserving the America Washington founded as a nation of innovators and entrepreneurs.

ACKNOWLEDGMENTS

◦→▰▶ ◀▰←◦

This book tells the story of the founder of our country and the private enterprises he founded. So let me begin the acknowledgments by sharing my gratitude to another founder of a great institution.

In 1984, Fred L. Smith, Jr., was a public policy entrepreneur founding a startup then headquartered in the kitchen of the apartment belonging to him and his wife, Fran, in the historic U Street area of Washington, DC, before the neighborhood became trendy. The startup was a new think tank called the Competitive Enterprise Institute, which would look at contemporary problems and then find and promote solutions inspired by America's founding fathers and the scholars through the ages who spread the ideas of liberty and permissionless private-sector innovation. A former political liberal who is justly proud of leading sit-ins in the 1960s as a college student in Louisiana, Fred remains a libertarian with an egalitarian mindset, still yearning to slash red tape for the purpose of giving opportunities to all. He has inspired countless individuals to take up the cause of restraining big-government regulation that thwarts the plans for advancement of millions of American entrepreneurs, investors, consumers, and families.

I am one of those Fred has inspired, and for the past 15 years, I have also been employed at the organization he started: CEI. I thank Fred for bringing me on-board at CEI for the one-year media fellowship—as I had been a journalist and staff writer for publications such as *Investor's Business Daily* and *Insight* magazine of the *Washington Times*—that has turned into 15 years of gainful employment at CEI studying the processes of innovation and entrepreneurship and how they interact with public policy. Fred, who is now chairman emeritus of CEI, and Fran—a brilliant policy scholar in her own right, who serves as Fred's proxy on our board (and who was my first DC boss at the policy group Consumer Alert)—continue to show incredible kindness to me and have been very encouraging about this book.

Also very encouraging about this book and all my policy endeavors is CEI's current president, Kent Lassman. Kent inspires my colleagues and me daily with his big-picture vision of advancing liberty and his specific, unique knowledge of trends in technology and innovation. Much encouragement has also come from Iain Murray, director of CEI's Center for Economic Freedom, and I have also benefitted greatly from Iain's vast historical knowledge of his native United Kingdom. Sam Kazman, Wayne Crews, Matthew Adams, Christine Hall, Amanda France, R. J. Smith, and so many other of my colleagues at CEI have provided friendship and invaluable insights that have made it into this book. I regret I can't name them all here, but hopefully they know who they are, and I will have the opportunity to tell them my thanks in an individual capacity.

I should note, however, that though my colleagues did provide me with many ideas utilized in this book, the opinions and observations expressed in these pages are mine alone and do not necessarily reflect the specific policy positions of CEI, nor of any other individuals that I acknowledge here in thanks. And there are so many wonderful people I need to thank.

The genesis of this book was a series of articles I would write each year for various publications around the time of George Washington's birthday. My friend Jennifer Cohen had the foresight to see that the story of George Washington's entrepreneurship could be a compelling book. As my agent, she helped me fashion several book proposals and became a tireless advocate in pitching them. She has continued to inspire me with good ideas throughout the publication process.

I thank Adam Bellow for selecting me to join the distinguished roster of authors he signed to All Points Books, his publishing imprint at St. Martin's Press. My writing of this book also benefitted from Adam's keen insights stemming from years of experience in the publishing world. During the editing process, I was also guided by the gentle hand and wise observations of St. Martin's assistant editor Kevin Reilly. Copy editors Jennifer Fernandez and Jennifer Simington also did an awesome job helping format my manuscript into attractive book form.

And I thank in advance the great St. Martin's publicity team of Leah Johanson, Sara Beth Haring, and Mac Nicholas, who have already shown they care about giving this book as wide a reach as possible.

Also exceedingly kind and helpful were the various associates of George Washington's Mount Vernon with whom I had the pleasure of working. Melissa Wood, Mount Vernon's director of communications, answered my many questions or put me in touch with on-staff experts who could. Samantha Snyder made me feel welcome doing research at the recently built Fred W. Smith (no relation to CEI founder Fred L. Smith—that we know of) National Library for the Study of George Washington. Doug Bradburn gave me a lengthy interview about the purpose of the modern Mount Vernon just a couple of weeks before the announcement of his promotion from director of the library to president and CEO of Mount Vernon in its entirety. Dawn Bonner, manager of visual resources, patiently went over with me many of the historic photos and images from Mount Vernon's archive and informed me of the places at which I could find others relating to the lives of George and Martha Washington. And longtime Mount Vernon staff historian Mary Thompson—a walking encyclopedia of details of the lives of George and Martha Washington—patiently answered my questions about basic facts and the context of the Washingtons' endeavors.

The talented photographer Kristen H. Murray took hundreds of beautiful photos on a sunny but cool day at Mount Vernon in December 2019. I regret that we could only use but a few of them in this book but urge readers to view her photos of Mount Vernon and other beautiful places and people on Instagram at @gardenographer, on Facebook at Gardenography by Kris, or on ViewBug at www.viewbug.com/member/gardenographer.

The fate of the great American experiment by Washington and his colleagues ultimately resides in the youngest generations. Will they preserve the flames of liberty kindled by Washington and our nation's founders, or move this country further toward socialism or other forms of collectivism and cronyism? That answer has yet to be delivered, but the talented young people who assisted in the writing of this book give me many reasons for hope. Zachary Frey—whose parents, Bill and Carrie, are also longtime friends—gave me invaluable assistance in researching this book when he interned for me in the summer of 2017. At the book's later stages, Gibson Kirsch, my intern in the fall and winter of 2019–20, gave me some great ideas for photos and images and made many other constructive suggestions.

I also learned quite a bit hanging out with my awesome niece and nephew Kaitlyn and Carter Batdorf, who are now, respectively, 13 and 11. They asked some good questions about George Washington's life and introduced me to the "Money Grandma" episode of *Teen Titans Go!*, in which Washington was brought back from the past to fight comical superheroes. Despite the wild storyline, the depiction of Washington as a person—tall, well-spoken, and a great marksman—was amazingly on the mark!

I also received a lot of support and words of encouragement from their parents, my sister and brother-in-law, Nancy and Eric Batdorf. And my dearest mother,

Marcia Berlau, has been an endless source of wisdom, understanding, and love my entire life. Ditto for my late father, Harry, to whom this book is dedicated. And my great-uncle Manuel Nowick—who has seen much history as a World War II combat veteran, radio actor, and civil rights attorney—continues to serve as an inspiration to me in his 100th year.

In addition to the associates of Mount Vernon, I received assistance from some wonderful people who are keeping alive traditions in which Washington participated. On Washington's early profession and lifelong vocation of land surveying, Curtis Sumner, executive director of the National Society of Professional Surveyors, gave me a superb overview of the way surveying has changed and the way it has not since Washington's time. Mark Tabbert, director of collections for the George Washington Masonic National Memorial Association in Alexandria, Virginia, answered many queries from me about Freemasons in Washington's day and in contemporary times.

Also in Alexandria, I had the pleasure of walking through the rooms of Gadsby's Tavern—a historic gathering place for the founding fathers that is now split between a museum and a working restaurant that serves eighteenth-century and contemporary fare. Museum director Liz Williams was very helpful, as was Katie Thomason, a young participant—wise beyond her preteen years—in Gadsby's Junior Docent program who took the other visitors and me through the historic tavern and explained the significance of the rooms and the objects in them. Through emails facilitated by Liz and her colleagues and Katie's parents, Frank Thomason and Nancy Butler, Katie sent me questions she wanted to see answered in the book. I've answered some of them, such as what books Washington read and what games he played. Once again, someone in the younger generation was very helpful, so thank you, Katie, and I hope you enjoy the book!

Of course, it can seem like yesterday that my generation—GenX—*was* the younger generation. I continue to stay in touch with some wonderful teachers I had in high school and college who inspired me to study history and to write. At Shawnee Mission East High School in the Kansas City suburb of Prairie Village, Kansas, I was especially fortunate to benefit from the wisdom and guidance of my counselor Deb Atkinson, my English teacher Nancy "Debe" Bramley, who spotted and nurtured my talent for writing, and my U.S. history teacher Karl Englund. I still have a vivid picture in my mind of Mr. Englund standing on desks to demonstrate the battles of various wars. Hope you all enjoy this book, and know that this is what you've wrought, for better or for worse!

From KC to DC, and points beyond and in between, I have a great group of friends that gave me encouragement and helpful advice. Thanks to Susan and Jim Archer, Al and Camelia Canata, Kaye Chase, Barbara and Ken Davidson, Bill and Jean Dunn, Mark Fortner, Tom and the late Janet Grow, Johnny McGuire, Tom and Jacque McGuire, Kevin Mooney, David Ozgo, Mitzi Perdue, Wes Seaton, Norm Singleton, Cynthia and Scott Stanley, Chris and Carol Thomas, Symeon and Merve Williams, and Tom Woodbury.

Finally, to my girlfriend, M.J. Carter, thank you for the comfort, encouragement, inspiration, and many good ideas you provided to me throughout this laborious writing process. I love you, Baby!!

APPENDIX

A SELECTION OF WASHINGTON'S BUSINESS CORRESPONDENCE

In his pioneering 1996 character study of George Washington, *Founding Father: Rediscovering George Washington,* Richard Brookhiser says that "Washington does not belong to the lively, but untrustworthy category of the speaking dead." His writings are not of the type from which we can take many bumper-sticker slogans. Rather, Brookhiser points out, Washington "wrote to respond to demands and get things done."[1]

But in some ways, Washington's writings are the more rewarding because they are so personal and detailed. We can glean from them the way his mind worked, along with insights on how to deal with friendships, family relationships, complex business transactions, and preserving the liberties of our country.

* * *

LETTER FROM GEORGE WASHINGTON TO ROBERT CARY & COMPANY, MAY 28, 1762

In this letter to Robert Cary & Company, the merchant firm in London that is Washington's agent for selling his tobacco crop, Washington expresses bewilderment and displeasure that his tobacco isn't getting a much better price, despite the improvements he made in cultivation. "Tobo" is short for tobacco.

To Robert Cary & Company

Mount Vernon 28th May 1762

Gentlemen,

Your unacknowledged favours of the 26th June 10th Augt 16 & 19th Septr and the 19th of Octr following now lye before—in that one of Augt 10th I perceive you bring the shortness of some of the Bundles of the Tobo Shipped in the Bland to acct for the lowness of the Price—That some of the Tobo was small I shall not undertake to dispute, but at the sametime I must observe that it was clean & neatly handled which I apprehended woud have rendered the other objection of very little weight—As to stemming my Tobo in the manner you recommend I woud readily do it if the returns woud be equivalent to the trouble, & loss of the Stem, and of this I shall be a tolerable judge as I am at no small pains this year to try the quality with the advantages & disadvantages of different kinds of Tobos and shall at the sametime find out the difference between a hhd of Leaf & a hhd of Stemmd Tobo by comparing then the loss of the one with the extra price of the other I shall be able to determine which is the best to pursue

& follow that method which promises the most certain advantages.

Some of the Tobo which I put on board the Unity Captn Cuzzens got damaged in carrying to the Warehouses for Inspection & had a part cut of which will no doubt deface it a little but as this happened while I was at Williamsburg I am able to give you no exact Information concerning it—In this parcel of Tobo there are three kinds which please to give me yr opinions upon—No. 1 to 6 Inclusive are of one kind—from 9 to 14 are of another—& 15 & 16 are of a third sort—the rest are of the same kinds of these three but made on other Plantations.

As I have ever laid it down as an established Maxim to believe that every person is, (most certainly ought to be) the best judges of What relates to their own Interest & Concerns I very rarely undertake to propose Schemes to others which may be attended with uncertainty & miscarriage—this will at once acct for my being among the last who shoud advise your sending a Vessell into Potomack for the accomodation of your Friends there. That I have often thought of it as a desirable thing for the Shippers, I will readily confess and have as often concluded that sosoon as you found an established consignment formed here you woud do it of course—and sooner we ought not to expect it—Since you have proposed the matter yourself to me—I certainly must approve of it, and as you are so obliging to write that you shall direct the Matter to be under my notice I hope you will be perswaded to believe that I shall readily contribute my best advice and assistance towards his dispatch—The Tobacco's of most of your friends upon Potomack (or that

Ships from thence) lyes within 15 Miles above & below this place, and as good, or the best harbour (Piscataway) is within sight of my Door—It has this great advantage besides good Anchorage & laying safe from the Winds that it is out of the way of the Worm which is very hurtful to Shipping a little lower down & lyes in a very plentiful part of the Country—I thought it incumbant upon me to mention these things after which do as you please. If I had receivd any Intimation of your sending a Vessell into this River I shoud not have engaged any part of my Tobo to Cuzzens, & while I remain in expectation of her arrival will not seek a freight else where for the residue of what I intend your house from this River which probably may amount to about 30 hhds more.

My Letter of the 25th of Jany will inform you how the Interest of the Bank stock is to be applied—as that fund was appropriated towards the payment of Miss Custis's Fortune I am informed that the Stock ought to be trans-ferred to her. you will please therefore to have it done accordingly and whatever charges may arise in so doing place to her own Acct. I hope Messrs Hill & Co. will send the wine into this River for I had rather have it in Madeira than York.

Thus far had I wrote & was going to conclude when your favour of the 18th Jany was presented to me—I am sorry to hear the Accts given of the Tobo Shipped in Boyes but as you don't particularize the proprietor's names who suffered most I am in hopes my 70 hhds have pretty well escaped the ge[ne]r[a]l complaint—If it has not I confess it to be an Art beyond my skill, to succeed in making good Tobo as I have used my utmost endeavours for that purpose this two or 3 years past—& am once again urged to express my surprize at finding that I do not partake of the best prices that are going—I saw an Acct rendered by Mr Athaws of some Tobo which he sold for Mr Fairfax at 12½d. the Tobo went from this River & I can aver was not better than 12 hhds of my Mountn Crop which you receivd in the Sarah & Bland last Summr—In fact Mr Fairfax's Plantation's & mine upon Shannondoah lye in the same neighbourhood—The Tobo brought to the same Inspection—and to be short, is in all respects exactly alike—none of mine however sold for more than 11d. or 3½ which you please while his went of a little before at the price of 12½ aforesaid—this is a difference really too great & I see it with concern—however Gentlemen I hope to find it otherwise for the time to come. I am Yr Most Obedt Hble Servt.

LETTER FROM GEORGE WASHINGTON TO ROBERT CARY & COMPANY, SEPTEMBER 20, 1765

In this letter to the Cary firm, Washington announces that he is phasing out his tobacco crop and asks Cary about the London price of hemp, which he is planning to grow as a replacement. This is also one of the first instances of Washington speaking out against the Stamp Act.

To Robert Cary & Company
Mount Vernon 20th September 1765.
Gentn
It cannot reasonably be imagined that I felt any pleasing Sensations upon the receipt of your Letter of the 13th of

February covering accts of Sales for 153 Hhds of Master Custis's Tobo and 115 of mine.

That the Sales are pitifully low, needs no words to demonstrate—and that they are worse than many of my Acquaintance upon this River—Potomack—have got in the Out Posts, & from Mr Russel and other Merchants of London for common Aronoko Tobo, is a truth equally as certain—Nay not so good as I myself have got from Mr Gildart of Liverpool for light Rent Tobaccos (shipd him at the same time I did to you) of the meanest sort; such as you once complaind of as the worst of Maryland & not Saleable—Can it be otherwise than a little mortifying then to find, that we, who raise none but Sweetscented Tobacco, and endeavour I may venture to add, to be careful in the management of it, however we fail in the execution, & who by a close and fixed corrispondance with you, contribute so largely to the dispatch of your Ships in this Country shoud meet with such unprofitable returns? Surely I may answer No! Notwithstanding, you will again receive my own Crops this year, & 67 Hhds of Master Custis's; but Gentlemen you must excuse me for adding (As I cannot readily conceive that our Tobacco's are so much depreciated in quality as not only to sell much below other Marks of good repute, but actually for less, as I before observd, than the commonest kinds do) that justice to myself & ward will render it absolutely necessary for me to change my corrispondance unless I experience an alteration for the better.

I might take notice upon this occasion also, that my Tobo Netts a good deal less than Master Custis's, & why it shoud do so, I am really at a loss to discover: his 153 Hhds averaging £7.7.7 and my 115 only £5.17.6—perhaps it may be urged that some of mine was Potomack Tobacco, I grant it, but take these out and the Yorks then average £6.6.5 only—If you had allowed him the benefit of the Bonded Duties I shoud not have wonderd at the difference, but this I perceive is not done, and certain I am, my Tobacco ought not to have been inferior to his—in any respect—the Lands being the same, & my directions for making it good equally as express.

Tobacco I well perceive for a year or two past, had fallen in its value—from what causes I shall not take upon me to determine—and I am not so extravagent as to believe that my own and Master Custis's Crops shoud fetch their usual prices when other good Tobacco met with abatements; but I am really selfish enough to expect that we ought to come in for a part of the good prices that are going, from a belief that our Tobacco is of a quality not so much inferior to some that still sells well, and that so considerable a Consignment—when confined in a manner to one House, as ours is—woud lay claim to the best endeavours of the Merchant in the Sales, and in the return of Goods, for many Articles of which I pay exceeding heavily. another thing I cannot easily Account for, unless it is on a Presumption that they are bought at very long credits which by no means ought to be the case; for where a Person has money in a Merchants hands he shoud doubtless have all the benefits that can result from that money—and in like manner where he pays Interest for the use of the Merchants shoud he be entitled to the same advantages, otherwise it might well be asked for what purpose is it that Interest is paid? Once upon my urging a complaint of this nature you wrote me, that the Goods ought to be sent back, and they shoud be returnd upon the Shopkeepers hands in cases of Imposition; but a moments reflection points out the Inconveniencies of such a measure unless (the Imposition be grossly abusive, or that) we coud afford to have a years stock before hand; how otherwise can a Person who Imports bear requisites only submit to lay a year out of any particular Article of Cloathing, or necessary for Family use, and have recourse to such a tedious & uncertain way of relief as this, when possibly a Tradesman woud deny the Goods & consequently refuse them—It is not to be done—we are obliged to acquiesce to the present loss & hope for future redress.

These Gentlemen are my Sentiments, fully, and candidly expressd, without any design—believe me—of giving you offence; but as the selling of our Tobacco's well, & purchasing of Our Goods upon the best Terms, are matters of the utmost consequence to our well doing, it behooves me to be plain and sincere in my declaration's on these points—previous to any change of measures—that I may stand acquitted of the Imputation of fickleness if I am at last forced to a discontinuance of my corrispondance with your House.

Twenty Hhds of my Tobacco from this River makes up Forty eight which I have in Boyes; the remainder (which is trifling) shall be sent by the first Ship that gives liberty; and as I have not been able to discover any advantages we obtaind by our Tobaccos lying so long upon hand, unsold, I shoud be glad to have the present Crops (& so of others if more be sent) disposd of to the first good

Chapmen, & the Sales returnd, unless there is a very probable certainty of a rise of price to warrant the keeping of it.

By this conveyance you will receive Invoices of Goods wanted for our Plantation's on York; and those for this River, will no longer I hope be sent in by Boyes for when they come into that River we really suffer by the strange mistakes that continually happen—Last year several parcels of Goods designd for York River were sent to this place and others for me left down there & in going backwards & forwards some were lost (things too of no inconsiderable value, for one of the parcels was a Bale of Linnen) and this year all my Plaid hose for this River came in a package to Mr Valentine & I have them to send for 150 Miles—These mistakes & Inconveniencies woud necessarily be avoided if the Goods were to come by Ships to the respective Rivers; and they woud also escape those frequent damages which is the consequence of shifting them from one Vessel to another, and transporting them from place to place—Oppertunities of doing this cannot be wanting as many Vessels comes to this River annually (from London) some of which lye at my Door.

It appears pretty evident to me from the prices I have generally got for my Tobacco in London, & from some other concomitant Circumstances, that it only suits the Interest of a few particular Gentlemen to continue their consignments of this commodity to that place, while others shoud endeavour to substitute some other Article in place of Tobacco, and try their success therewith. In order thereto you woud do me a singular favour in advising of the general price one might expect for good

Hemp in your Port watered & prepared according to Act of Parliament, with an estimate of the freight, & all other Incident charges pr Tonn that I may form some Idea of the profits resulting from the growth—I shoud be very glad to know at the sametime how rough & undressd Flax has generally, and may probably sell; for this year I have made an Essay in both, and altho. I suffer pretty considerably by the attempt, owing principally to the severity of the Drought, & my inexperience in the management I am not altogether discouraged from a further prosecution of the Scheme provided I find the Sales with you are not clogd with too much difficulty and expence.

The Stamp Act, imposed on the Colonies by the Parliament of Great Britain engrosses the conversation of the speculative part of the Colonists, who look upon this unconstitutional method of Taxation as a direful attack upon their Liberties, & loudly exclaim against the violation—What may be the result of this (I think I may add) ill Judgd measure, and the late restrictions of our Trade and other Acts to Burthen us, I will not undertake to determine; but this I think may be said—that the advantages accruing to the Mother Country will fall far short of the expectation's of the Ministry; for certain it is, that the whole produce of our labour hitherto has centred in Great Britain—what more can they desire? and that all Taxes which contribute to lessen our Importation of British Goods must be hurtful to the Manufacturers of them, and to the Common Weal—The Eyes of our People (already beginning to open) will perceive, that many of the Luxuries which we have heretofore lavished our Substance to Great Britain for can well be dispensed with whilst the Necessaries of Life are to be procurd (for the most part) within ourselves—This consequently will introduce frugality; and be a necessary stimulation to Industry—Great Britain may then load her Exports with as Heavy Taxes as She pleases but where will the consumption be? I am apt to think no Law or usage can compel us to barter our money or Staple Commodities for their Manufactures, if we can be supplied within ourselve upon the better Terms—nor will her Traders dispose of them without a valuable consideration and surety of Pay—where then lyes the utility of these Measures?

As to the Stamp Act taken in a single and distinct view; one, & the first bad consequence attending of it I take to be this—our Courts of Judicature will be shut up, it being morally impossible under our present Circumstances that the Act of Parliament can be complied with, were we ever so willing to enforce the execution; for not to say, which alone woud be sufficient, that there is not money to pay the Stamps there are many other Cogent Reasons to prevent it and if a stop be put to our Judicial proceedings it may be left to yourselves, who have such large demands upon the Colonies, to determine, who is to suffer most in this event—the Merchant, or the Planter.

I am very much obliged to you for your kind advice of corrisponding with Mr Dandridge—it is a piece of respect due to so near a Relation of my Wifes, & therefore I give you the trouble of the Inclosed; but I have not the least expectation of deriving any advantages from it for thô he has no nearer relatives than her, there are some to whom I believe he has given stronger proofs of his Inclinations of serving—but to you my thanks are equaly due,

& I return them with cordiality for the goodness of your Intentions. I am Gentn Yr Most Obedt h[umbl]e Servt

Go: Washington

LETTER FROM GEORGE WASHINGTON TO GEORGE MASON, APRIL 5, 1769

This letter from Washington to his Fairfax County neighbor George Mason, then a fellow member of the Virginia House of Burgesses, is one of the most historically significant letters he ever wrote. James Thomas Flexner called it "a major milestone of Washington's road to Revolution."[2] Speaking specifically of his gristmill and other manufacturing enterprises, Washington reasoned that for Great Britain, it was "no greater hardship to forbid my manufacturing, than it is to order me to buy Goods of them loaded with Duties, for the express purpose of raising a revenue."

Mason would later co-author with Washington the Fairfax Resolves in 1774 and author the Virginia Declaration of Rights in 1776. These documents influenced greatly both the Declaration of Independence and the Bill of Rights of the U.S. Constitution.

To George Mason
Mount Vernon 5th April 1769.
Dear sir,
Herewith you will receive a letter and sundry papers which were forwarded to me a day or two ago by Doctor Ross of Bladensburg. I transmit them with the greater pleasure, as my own desire of knowing your sentiments

upon a matter of this importance exactly coincides with the Doctrs inclinations.

At a time when our lordly Masters in Great Britain will be satisfied with nothing less than the deprivation of American freedom, it seems highly necessary that something shou'd be done to avert the stroke and maintain the liberty which we have derived from our Ancestors; but the manner of doing it to answer the purpose effectually is the point in question.

That no man shou'd scruple, or hesitate a moment to use a—ms in defence of so valuable a blessing, on which all the good and evil of life depends; is clearly my opinion; Yet A—ms I wou'd beg leave to add, should be the last resource; the de[r]nier resort. Addresses to the Throne, and remonstrances to parliament, we have already, it is said, proved the inefficacy of; how far then their attention to our rights & priviledges is to be awakened or alarmed by starving their Trade & manufactures, remains to be tryed.

The northern Colonies, it appears, are endeavouring to adopt this scheme—In my opinion it is a good one; & must be attended with salutary effects, provided it can be carried pretty generally into execution; but how far it is practicable to do so, I will not take upon me to determine. That there will be difficulties attending the execution of it every where, from clashing interests, & selfish designing men (ever attentive to their own gain, & watchful of every turn that can assist their lucrative views, in preference to any other consideration) cannot be denied; but in the Tobacco Colonies where the Trade is so diffused, and in a manner wholly conducted by Factors for their principals at home, these difficulties are certainly enhanced, but I think not insurmountably increased, if the Gentlemen in their several counties wou'd be at some pains to explain matters to the people, & stimulate them to a cordial agreement to purchase none but certain innumerated articles out of any of the Stores after such a period, nor import nor purchase any themselves. This, if it did not effectually withdraw the Factors from their Importations, wou'd at least make them extremely cautious in doing it, as the prohibited Goods could be vended to none but the non-associater, or those who wou'd pay no regard to their association; both of whom ought to be stigmatized, and made the objects of publick reproach.

The more I consider a Scheme of this sort, the more ardently I wish success to it, because I think there are private, as well as public advantages to result from it—the former certain, however precarious the other may prove; for in respect to the latter I have always thought that by virtue of the same power (for here alone the authority derives) which assume's the right of Taxation, they may attempt at least to restrain our manufactories; especially those of a public nature; the same equity & justice prevailing in the one case as the other, it being no greater hardship to forbid my manufacturing, than it is to order me to buy Goods of them loaded with Duties, for the express purpose of raising a revenue. But as a measure of this sort will be an additional exertion of arbitrary power, we cannot be worsted I think in putting it to the Test. On the other hand, that the Colonies are considerably indebted to Great Britain, is a truth universally acknowledged. That many families are reduced, almost, if not quite, to penury

& want, from the low ebb of their fortunes, and Estates daily selling for the discharge of Debts, the public papers furnish but too many melancholy proofs of. And that a scheme of this sort will contribute more effectually than any other I can devise to immerge the Country from the distress it at present labours under, I do most firmly believe, if it can be generally adopted. And I can see but one set of people (the Merchants excepted) who will not, or ought not, to wish well to the Scheme; and that is those who live genteely & hospitably, on clear Estates. Such as these were they, not to consider the valuable object in view, & the good of others, might think it hard to be curtail'd in their living & enjoyments; for as to the penurious man, he saves his money, & he saves his credit; having the best plea for doing that, which before perhaps he had the most violent struggles to refrain from doing. The extravagant & expensive man has the same good plea to retrench his Expences—He is thereby furnished with a pretext to live within bounds, and embraces it—prudence dictated œconomy to him before, but his resolution was too weak to put it in practice; for how can I, *says he*, who have lived in such & such a manner change my method? I am ashamed to do it: and besides, such an alteration in the System of my living, will create suspicions of a decay in my fortune, & such a thought the world must not harbour; I will e'en continue my course: till at last the course discontinues the Estate, a sale of it being the consequence of his perseverance in error. This I am satisfied is the way that many who have set out in the wrong tract, have reasoned, till ruin stares them in the face. And in respect to the poor & needy man, he is only left in the same situation he was found; better I might say, because as he judges from comparison, his condition is amended in proportion as it approaches nearer to those above him.

Upon the whole therefore, I think the Scheme a good one, and that it ought to be tryed here, with such alterations as the exigency of our circumstances render absolutely necessary; but how, & in what manner to begin the work, is a matter worthy of consideration; and whether it can be attempted with propriety, or efficacy (further than a communication of sentiments to one another) before May, when the Court & Assembly will meet together in Williamsburg, and a uniform plan can be concerted, and sent into the different counties to operate at the same time, & in the same manner every where, is a thing I am somewhat in doubt upon, & shou'd be glad to know your opinion of. I am Dr Sir Your most Obt humble Servant

G: Washington

FAIRFAX [COUNTY] RESOLVES, JULY 18, 1774

In July 1774, shortly after Virginia's royal governor shut down the House of Burgesses for issuing a proclamation against the British government, Washington sat down at Mount Vernon with his neighbor George Mason, and wrote what has come to be known as the "Fairfax Resolves." Written with the intent of rousing the colonists in the fight for economic—if not yet political—independence from Great Britain, the document contained 24 statements each beginning with the word "Resolved." The Resolves were presented at a meeting of Fairfax County property owners, where they were enthusiastically approved and signed by 25 of the county's leading residents, including Washington and Mason. They were presented to the Continental Congress later that year.

The Resolves are a mixture of complaints against the British government, proclamations of natural rights, and calls to defy British regulations on manufacturing. The document is also notable for calling on Great Britain to temporarily halt and work to end the slave trade in the colonies. In unusually blunt terms for the time and place, the Resolves call the slave trade "a wicked cruel and unnatural Trade." This is the only known instance in which Washington expressed his growing antipathy toward slavery in public, although he would later do so in many private letters and would free all his slaves in his will.

At a general Meeting of the Freeholders and Inhabitants of the County of Fairfax on Monday the 18th day of July 1774, at the Court House, George Washington Esquire Chairman, and Robert Harrison Gent. Clerk of the said Meeting—

1. Resolved that this Colony and Dominion of Virginia can not be considered as a conquered Country; and if it was, that the present Inhabitants are the Descendants not of the Conquered, but of the Conquerors. That the same was not setled at the national Expence of England, but at the private Expence of the Adventurers, our Ancestors, by solemn Compact with, and under the Auspices and Protection of the British Crown; upon which we are in every Respect as dependant, as the People of Great Britain, and in the same Manner subject to all

his Majesty's just, legal, and constitutional Prerogatives. That our Ancestors, when they left their native Land, and setled in America, brought with them (even if the same had not been confirmed by Charters) the Civil-Constitution and Form of Government of the Country they came from; and were by the Laws of Nature and Nations, entitled to all it's Privileges, Immunities and Advantages; which have descended to us their Posterity, and ought of Right to be as fully enjoyed, as if we had still continued within the Realm of England.

2. Resolved that the most important and valuable Part of the British Constitution, upon which it's very Existence depends, is the fundamental Principle of the People's being governed by no Laws, to which they have not given their Consent, by Representatives freely chosen by them-selves; who are affected by the Laws they enact equally with their Constituents; to whom they are accountable, and whose Burthens they share; in which consists the Safety and Happiness of the Community: for if this Part of the Constitution was taken away, or materially altered, the Government must degenerate either into an abso-lute and despotic Monarchy, or a tyrannical Aristocracy, and the Freedom of the People be annihilated.

3. Resolved therefore, as the Inhabitants of the american Colonies are not, and from their situation can not be represented in the British Parliament, that the leg-islative Power here can of Right be exercised only by our own Provincial Assemblys or Parliaments, subject to the Assent or Negative of the British Crown, to be declared within some proper limited Time. But as it was thought just and reasonable that the People of

Great Britain shou'd reap Advantages from these Colonies adequate to the Protection they afforded them, the British Parliament have claimed and exercised the Power of regulating our Trade and Commerce, so as to restrain our importing from foreign Countrys, such Articles as they cou'd furnish us with, of their own Growth or Manufacture, or exporting to foreign Countrys such Articles and Portions of our Produce, as Great Britain stood in Need of, for her own Consumption or Manufactures. Such a Power directed with Wisdom and Moderation, seems necessary for the general Good of that great Body-politic of which we are a Part; altho' in some Degree repugnant to the Principles of the Constitution. Under this Idea our Ancestors submitted to it: the Experience of more than a Century, during the government of the reciprocal Benefits flowing from it produced mutual uninterrupted Harmony and Good-Will, between the Inhabitants of Great Britain and her Colonies; who during that long Period, always considered themselves as one and same People: and tho' such a Power is capable of Abuse, and in some Instances hath been stretched beyond the original Design and Institution. Yet to avoid Strife and Contention with our fellow-Subjects, and strongly impressed with the Experience of mutual Benefits, we always Chearfully acquiesced in it, while the entire Regulation of our internal Policy, and giving and granting our own Money were preserved to our own provincial Legislatures.

4. Resolved that it is the Duty of these Colonies, on all Emergencies, to contribute, in Proportion to their Abilities, Situation and Circumstances, to the necessary

Charge of supporting and defending the British Empire, of which they are Part; that while we are treated upon an equal Footing with our fellow Subjects, the Motives of Self-Interest and Preservation will be a sufficient Obligation; as was evident thro' the Course of the last War; and that no Argument can be fairly applyed to the British Parliament's taxing us, upon a Presumption that we shou'd refuse a just and reasonable Contribution, but will equally operate in Justification of the Executive-Power taxing the People of England, upon a Supposition of their Representatives refusing to grant the necessary Supplies.

5. Resolved that the Claim lately assumed and exercised by the British Parliament, of making all such Laws as they think fit, to govern the People of these Colonies, and to extort from us our Money with out our Consent, is not only diametrically contrary to the first Principles of the Constitution, and the original Compacts by which we are dependant upon the British Crown and Government; but is totally incompatible with the Privileges of a free People, and the natural Rights of Mankind; will render our own Legislatures merely nominal and nugatory, and is calculated to reduce us from a State of Freedom and Happiness to Slavery and Misery.

6. Resolved that Taxation and Representation are in their Nature inseperable; that the Right of withholding, or of giving and granting their own Money is the only effectual Security to a free People, against the Incroachments of Despotism and Tyranny; and that whenever they yield the One, they must quickly fall a Prey to the other.

7. Resolved that the Powers over the People of America now claimed by the British House of Commons, in whose Election we have no Share, on whose Determinations we can have no Influence, whose Information must be always defective and often false, who in many Instances may have a seperate, and in some an opposite Interest to ours, and who are removed from those Impressions of tenderness and compassion arising from personal intercourse and Connections, which soften the Rigours of the most despotic Governments, must if continued, establish the most grievous and intollerable Species of Tyranny and Oppression, that ever was inflicted upon Mankind.

8. Resolved that it is our greatest Wish and Inclination, as well as Interest, to continue our Connection with, and Dependance upon the British Government; but tho' we are it's Subjects, we will use every Means which Heaven hath given us to prevent our becoming it's Slaves.

9. Resolved that there is a premeditated Design and System, formed and pursued by the British Ministry, to introduce an arbitrary Government into his Majesty's American Diminions; to which End they are artfully prejudicing our Sovereign, and inflaming the Minds of our fellow-Subjects in Great Britain, by propagating the most malevolent Falsehoods; particularly that there is an Intention in the American Colonies to set up for independant States; endeavouring at the same Time, by various Acts of Violence and Oppression, by sudden and repeated Dissolutions of our Assemblies, whenever they presume to examine the Illegality of ministerial Mandates, or deliberate on the violated Rights of their

Constituents, and by breaking in upon the American Charters, to reduce us to a State of Desperation, and dissolve the original Compacts by which our Ancestors bound themselves and their Posterity to remain dependant upon the British Crown: which Measures, unless effectually counteracted, will end in the Ruin both of Great Britain and her Colonies.

10. Resolved that the several Acts of Parliament for raising a Revenue upon the People of America without their Consent, the creating new and dangerous Jurisdictions here, the taking away our Trials by Jurys, the ordering Persons upon Criminal Accusations, to be tried in another Country than that in which the Fact is charged to have been committed, the Act inflicting ministerial Vengeance upon the Town of Boston, and the two Bills lately brought into Parliament for abrogating the Charter of the Province of Massachusetts Bay, and for the Protection and Encouragement of Murderers in the said Province, are Part of the above mentioned iniquitous System. That the Inhabitants of the Town of Boston are now suffering in the common Cause of all British America, and are justly entitled to it's Support and Assistance; and therefore that a Subscription ought imediatly to be opened, and proper Persons appointed, in every County of this Colony to purchase Provisions, and consign them to some Gentleman of Character in Boston, to be distributed among the poorer Sort of People there.

11. Resolved that we will cordially join with our Friends and Brethren of this and the other Colonies, in such Measures as shall be judged most effectual for procuring

Redress of our Grievances, and that upon obtaining such Redress if the Destruction of the Tea at Boston be regarded as an Invasion of private Property, we shall be willing to contribute towards paying the East India Company the Value: but as we consider the said Company as the Tools and Instrument of Oppression in the Hands of Government and the Cause of our present Distress, it is the Opinion of this Meeting that the People of these Colonies shou'd forbear all further Dealings with them, by refusing to purchase their Merchandize, until that Peace Safety and Good-order, which they have disturbed, be perfectly restored. And that all Tea now in this Colony, or which shall be imported into it shiped before the first Day of September next, shou'd be deposited in some Store-house to be appointed by the respective Committees of each County, until a sufficient Sum of Money be raised by Subscription to reimburse the Owners the Value, and then to be publickly burn'd and destroyed; and if the same is not paid for and destroyed as aforesaid, that it remain in the Custody of the said Committees, at the Risque of the Owners, until the Act of Parliament imposing a Duty upon Tea for raising a Revenue in America be repealed; and imediatly afterwards be delivered unto the several Proprietors thereof, their Agents or Attorneys.

12. Resolved that Nothing will so much contribute to defeat the pernicious Designs of the common Enemies of Great Britain and her Colonies as a firm Union of the latter; who ought to regard every Act of Violence or Oppression inflicted upon any one of them, as aimed at all; and to effect this desireable Purpose, that a Congress

shou'd be appointed, to consist of Deputies from all the Colonies, to concert a general and uniform Plan for the Defence and Preservation of our common Rights, and continueing the Connection and Dependance of the said Colonies upon Great Britain under a just, lenient, permanent, and constitutional Form of Government.

13. Resolved that our most sincere and cordial Thanks be given to the Patrons and Friends of Liberty in Great Britain, for their spirited and patriotick Conduct in Support of our constitutional Rights and Privileges, and their generous Efforts to prevent the present Distress and Calamity of America.

14. Resolved that every little jarring Interest and Dispute, which has ever happened between these Colonies, shou'd be buried in eternal Oblivion; that all Manner of Luxury and Extravagance ought imediatly to be laid aside, as totally inconsistent with the threatening and gloomy Prospect before us; that it is the indispensable Duty of all the Gentlemen and Men of Fortune to set Examples of Temperance, Fortitude, Frugality and Industry; and give every Encouragement in their Power, particularly by Subscriptions and Premiums, to the Improvement of Arts and Manufactures in America; that great Care and Attention shou'd be had to the Cultivation of Flax, Cotton, and other Materials for Manufactures; and we recommend it to such of the Inhabitants who have large Stocks of Sheep, to sell to their Neighbors at a moderate Price, as the most certain Means of speedily increasing our Breed of Sheep, and Quantity of Wool.

15. Resolved that until American Grievances be redressed, by Restoration of our just Rights and Privileges, no Goods or Merchandize whatsoever ought to be imported into this Colony, which shall be shiped from Great Britain or Ireland after the first Day of September next, except Linnens not exceeding fifteen Pence per yard, coarse woolen Cloth, not exceeding two Shillings sterling per Yard, Nails Wire, and Wire-Cards, Needles & Pins, Paper, Salt Petre, and Medecines; which may which three Articles only may be imported until the first Day of September, one thousand seven hundred and seventy six; and if any Goods or Merchandize, other than those hereby excepted, shou'd be ship'd from Great Britain or Ireland after the time aforesaid, to this Colony, that the same, immediately upon their Arrival, shou'd either be sent back again, by the Owners their Agents or Attorneys, or stored and deposited in some Ware-house, to be appointed by the Committee for each respective County, and there kept, at the Risque and Charge of the Owners, to be delivered to them, when a free Importation of Goods hither shall again take Place. And that the Merchants and Venders of Goods and Merchandize within this Colony ought not to take Advantage of our present Distress but continue to sell the Goods and Merchandize which they now have, or which may be shiped to them before the first Day of September next, at the same Rates and Prices they have been accustomed to do, within one Year last past; and if any Person shall sell such Goods on any other Terms than above expressed, that no Inhabitant of this Colony

shou'd at any time, for ever thereafter, deal with him, his Agent, Factor, or Store keepers for any Commodity whatsoever.

16. Resolved that it is the Opinion of this Meeting, that the Merchants and Venders of Goods and Merchandize within this Colony shou'd take an Oath, not to sell or dispose of any Goods or Merchandize whatsoever, which may be shiped from Great Britain or Ireland after the first Day of September next as aforesaid, except the Articles before excepted, and that they will, upon Receipt of such prohibited Goods, either send the same back again by the first Opportunity, or deliver them to the Committees in the respective Countys, to be deposited in some Warehouse, at the Risque and Charge of the Owners, until they, their Agents or Factors be permitted to take them away by the said Committees: the Names of those who refuse to take such Oath to be advertized by the respective Committees in the Countys wherein they reside. And to the End that the Inhabitants of this Colony may know what Merchants, and Venders of Goods and Merchandize have taken such Oath, that the respective Committees shou'd grant a Certificate thereof to every such Person who shall take the same.

17. Resolved that it is the Opinion of this Meeting, that during our present Difficulties and Distress, no Slaves ought to be imported into any of the British Colonies on this Continent; and we take this Opportunity of declaring our most earnest Wishes to see an entire Stop for ever put to such a wicked cruel and unnatural Trade.

18. Resolved that no kind of Lumber shou'd be exported

from this Colony to the West Indies, until America be restored to her constitutional Rights and Liberties if the other Colonies will accede to a like Resolution; and that it be recommended to the general Congress to appoint as early a Day as possible for stopping such Export.

19. Resolved that it is the Opinion of this Meeting, if American Grievances be not redressed before the first Day of November one thousand seven hundred and seventy five, that all Exports of Produce from the several Colonies to Great Britain [or Ireland] shou'd cease; and to carry the said Resolution more effectually into Execution, that we will not plant or cultivate any Tobacco, after the Crop now growing; provided the same Measure shall be adopted by the other Colonies on this Continent, as well those who have heretofore made Tobacco, as those who have n[o]t. And it is our Opinion also, if the Congress of Deputies from the several Colonies shall adopt the Measure of Non-exportation to Great Britain, as the People will be thereby disabled from paying their Debts, that no Judgements shou'd be rendered by the Courts in the said Colonies for any Debt, after Information of the said Measure's being determined upon.

20. Resolved that it is the Opinion of this Meeting that a solemn Covenant and Association shou'd be entered into by the Inhabitants of all the Colonies upon Oath, that they will not, after the Times which shall be respectively agreed on at the general Congress, export any Manner of Lumber to the West Indies, nor any of their Produce to Great Britain or Ireland, or sell or dispose

of the same to any Person who shall not have entered into the said Covenant and Association; and also that they will no import or receive any Goods or Merchandize which shall be ship'd from Great Britain or Ireland after the first Day of September next, other than the before enumerated Articles, nor buy or purchase any Goods, except as before excepted, of any Person whatsoever, who shall not have taken the Oath herein before recommended to be taken by the Merchants and Venders of Goods nor buy or purchase any Slaves hereafter imported into any Part of this Continent until a free Exportation and Importation be again resolved on by a Majority of the Representatives or Deputies of the Colonies. And that the respective Committees of the Countys, in each Colony so soon as the Covenant and Association becomes general, publich by Advertisements in their several Counties a List of the Names of those (if any such there be) who will not accede thereto; that such Traitors to their Country may be publickly known and detested.

21. Resolved that it is the Opinion of this Meeting, that this and the other associating Colonies shou'd break off all Trade, Intercourse, and Dealings, with that Colony Province or Town which shall decline or refuse to agree to the Plan which shall be adopted by the general Congress.

22. Resolved that shou'd the Town of Boston be forced to submit to the late cruel and oppressive Measures of Government, that we shall not hold the same to be binding upon us, but will, notwithstanding, religiously maintain, and inviolably adhere to such Measures as

shall be concerted by the general Congress, for the preservation of our Lives Liberties and Fortunes.

23. Resolved that it be recommended to the Deputies of the general Congress to draw up and transmit an humble and dutiful Petition and Remonstrance to his Majesty, asserting with decent Firmness our just and constitutional Rights and Privileg[es,] lamenting the fatal Necessity of being compelled to enter into Measur[es] disgusting to his Majesty and his Parliament, or injurious to our fellow Subjects in Great Britain; declaring, in the strongest Terms, ou[r] Duty and Affection to his Majesty's Person, Family [an]d Government, and our Desire to continue our Dependance upon Great Bri[tai]n; and most humbly conjuring and besecching his Majesty, not to reduce his faithful Subjects of America to a State of desperation, and to reflect, that from our Sovereign there can be but one Appeal. And it is the Opinion of this Meeting, that after such Petition and Remonstrance shall have been presented to his Majesty, the same shou'd be printed in the public Papers, in all the principal Towns in Great Britain.

24. Resolved that George Washington Esquire, and George Broadwater Gent. lately elected our Representatives to serve in the general Assembly, be appointed to attend the Convention at Williamsburg on the first Day of August next, and present these Resolves, as the Sense of the People of this County, upon the Measures proper to be taken in the present alarming and dangerous Situation of America.

✷ ✷ ✷

LETTERS FROM GEORGE WASHINGTON TO BRYAN FAIRFAX, JULY 1774

While the leaders of Fairfax County enthusiastically supported the Resolves, some members of the Fairfax family did not. Bryan Fairfax was the son of William and the younger brother of George William, both of whom had mentored the young George. Washington viewed the entire family with deep affection, so he was hurt that his stance had upset Bryan. In these letters written in July 1774, one before and one after Washington and Mason produced the Resolves, Washington tries to convince Fairfax that there is no other choice but drastic action against Great Britain.

To Bryan Fairfax

Mount Vernon, 4 July, 1774.

Dear Sir,

John has just delivered to me your favor of yesterday, which I shall be obliged to answer in a more concise manner, than I could wish, as I am very much engaged in raising one of the additions to my house, which I think (perhaps it is fancy) goes on better whilst I am present, than in my absence from the workmen.

I own to you, Sir, I wished much to hear of your making an open declaration of taking a poll for this county, upon Colonel West's publicly declining last Sunday; and I should have written to you on the subject, but for information then received from several gentlemen in the churchyard, of your having refused to do so, for the reasons assigned in your letter; upon which, as I think the country never stood more in need of men of abilities and liberal sentiments than now, I entreated several gentlemen at our church yesterday to press Colonel Mason to take a poll, as I really think Major Broadwater, though a good man, might do as well in the discharge of his domestic concerns, as in the capacity of a legislator. And therefore I again express my wish, that either you or Colonel Mason would offer. I can be of little assistance to either, because I early laid it down as a maxim not to propose myself, and solicit for a second.

As to your political sentiments, I would heartily join you in them, so far as relates to a humble and dutiful petition to the throne, provided there was the most distant hope of success. But have we not tried this already? Have we not addressed the Lords, and remonstrated to the Commons? And to what end? Did they deign to look at our petitions? Does it not appear, as clear as the sun in its meridian brightness, that there is a regular, systematic plan formed to fix the right and practice of taxation upon us? Does not the uniform conduct of Parliament for some years past confirm this? Do not all the debates, especially those just brought to us, in the House of Commons on the side of government, expressly declare that America must be taxed in aid of the British funds, and that she has no longer resources within herself? Is there any thing to be expected from petitioning after this? Is not the attack upon the liberty and property of the people of Boston, before restitution of the loss to the India Company was demanded, a plain and self-evident proof of what they are aiming at? Do not the subsequent bills (now I dare say acts), for depriving the Massachusetts Bay of its charter, and for transporting offenders into other colonies or to Great Britain for trial, where it is impossible from the nature of the thing that justice can be obtained, convince us that the administration is determined to stick at nothing to carry its point? Ought we not, then, to put our virtue and fortitude to the severest test?

With you I think it a folly to attempt more than we can execute, as that will not only bring disgrace upon us, but weaken our cause; yet I think we may do more than is generally believed, in respect to the non-importation scheme. As to the withholding of our remittances, that is another point, in which I own I have my doubts on several accounts, but principally on that of justice; for I think, whilst we are accusing others of injustice, we should be just ourselves; and how this can be, whilst we owe a considerable debt, and refuse payment of it to Great Britain, is to me inconceivable. Nothing but the last extremity, I think, can justify it. Whether this is now come, is the question.

I began with telling you, that I was to write a short letter. My paper informs me I have done otherwise. I shall hope to see you to-morrow, at the meeting of the county in Alexandria, when these points are to be considered. I am, dear Sir, your most obedient and humble servant.

✳ ✳ ✳

To Bryan Fairfax
Mount Vernon July 20th 1774.
Dear Sir,
Your Letter of the 17th was not presented to me till after the Resolution's (which were adjudg'd advisable for this

county to come to) had been revis'd, alterd, & corrected
in the Committee; nor till we had gone into a general
Meeting in the Court House, and my attention necessarily
call'd every moment to the business that was before it; I
did however upon receipt of it (in that hurry & bustle)
hastily run it over, and handed it round to the Gentlemen on the Bench, of which there were many; but as no
person present seem'd in the least disposed to adopt your
Sentiments—as there appeard a perfect satisfaction, & ac-
quiescence to the measures propos'd (except from a Mr
Williamson, who was for adopting your advise litterally,
without obtaining a Second voice on his Side)—and as
the Gentlemen to whom the Letter was shown, advis'd me
not to have it read, as it was not like to make a Convert, &
repugnant (some of them thought) to the very principle
we were contending for, I forebore to offer it otherwise
than in the manner abovementioned, which I shall be
sorry for, if it gives you any dissatisfaction in not having
your Sentiments read to the County at large, instead of
communicating them to the first People in it, by offering
them the Letter in the manner I did.

That I differ very widely from you, in respect to the
mode of obtaining a repeal of the Acts so much, & so
justly complaind of, I shall not hesitate to acknowledge;
& that this difference in opinion may, probably, proceed
from the different Construction's we put upon the Conduct, & Intention of the Ministry, may also be true; But
as I see nothing on the one hand, to induce a belief that
the Parliament would embrace a favourable oppertunity
of Repealing Acts which they go on with great rapidity to
pass, in order to enforce their Tyrannical System; and on

the other, observe, or think I observe, that Government is pursuing a regular Plan at the expence of Law & justice, to overthrow our Constitutional Rights & liberties, how can I expect any redress from a Measure which hath been ineffectually tryd already—For Sir what is it we are contending against? Is it against paying the duty of 3d. pr lb. on Tea because burthensome? No, it is the Right only, we have all along disputed, & to this end we have already Petitiond his Majesty in as humble, & dutiful a manner as Subjects could do; nay more, we applied to the House of Lords, & House of Commons in their different Legislative Capacities setting forth that, as Englishmen, we could not be deprivd of this essential, & valuable part of our Constitution; If then (as the Fact really is) it is against the Right of Taxation we now do, & (as I before said) all along have contended, why should they suppose an exertion of this power would be less obnoxious now, than formerly? and what reasons have we to believe that, they would make a Second attempt whilst the same Sentiments fill'd the Breast of every American, if they did not intend to inforce it if possible? The conduct of the Boston People could not justify the rigour of their Measures, unless their had been a requisition of payment & refusal of it; nor did that measure require an Act to deprive the Governmt of Massachusets Bay of their Charter; or to exempt Offenders from tryal in the place, where Offences were Committed, as there was not, nor could not be, a single Instance produced to manifest the necessity of it—Are not all these things self evident proofs of a fixed & uniform Plan to Tax us? If we want further proofs, does not all the Debates in the House of Commons serve to confirm this? and hath not Genl Gage's Conduct since his arrival (in Stopping the Address of his Council, & Publishing a Proclamation more becoming a Turkish Bashaw than an English Govr & declaring it Treason to associate in any manner by which the Commerce of Great Britain is to be affected) exhibited unexampled Testimony of the most despotick System of Tyranny that ever was practiced in a free Government. In short what further proofs are wanting to satisfy one of the design's of the Ministry than their own Acts; which are uniform, & plainly tending to the same point—nay, if I mistake not, avowedly to fix the Right of Taxation— what hope then from Petitioning, when they tell us that now, or never, is the time to fix the matter—shall we after this whine & cry for releif, when we have already tried it in vain?, or shall we supinely sit, and see one Provence after another fall a Sacrafice to Despotism? If I was in any doubt as to the Right wch the Parliament of Great Britain had to Tax us without our Consents, I should most heartily coincide with you in opinion, that to Petition, & petition only, is the proper method to apply for relief; because we should then be asking a favour, & not claiming a Right wch by the Law of Nature & our Constitution we are, in my opinion, indubitably entitled to; I should even think it criminal to go further than this, under such an Idea; but none such I have, I think the Parliament of Great Britain hath no more Right to put their hands into my Pocket, without my consent, than I have to put my hands into your's, for money; and this being already urged to them in a firm, but decent manner by all the

Colonies, what reason is there to expect any thing from their justice?

As to the Resolution for addressing the Throne, I own to you Sir I think the whole might as well have been expung'd; I expect nothing from the measure; nor shd my voice have accompanied it, if the non-Importation Scheme was intended to be Retarded by it; for I am convinc'd, as much as I am of my Existance, that there is no relief for us but in their distress; & I think, at least I hope, that there is publick Virtue enough left among us to deny ourselves every thing but the bare necessaries of Life to accomplish this end—this we have a Right to do, & no power upon Earth can compel us to do otherwise, till they have first reducd us to the most abject state of Slavery that ever was designd for Mankind. The Stopping our Exports would, no doubt, be a shorter Cut than the other, to effect this purpose, but if we owe Money to Great Britain, nothing but the last necessity can justify the Non-payment of it; and therefore, I have great doubts upon this head, & wish to see the other method, which is legal, & will facilitate these payments, first tried.

I cannot conclude, without expressing some concern that I should differ so widely in Sentiments from you in a matter of such great Moment, & general Import; & should much distrust my own judgment upon the occasion, if my Nature did not recoil at the thought of Submitting to Measures which I think Subversive of every thing that I ought to hold dear and valuable—and did I not find, at the sametime, that the voice of Mankind is with me. I must appologize for sending you so rough a sketch of my thoughts upon your Letter. when I look'd back and saw the length of my own, I could not, as I am also a good deal hurried at this time, bear the thoughts of making off a fair Copy. I am Dr Sir Yr Most Obedt Humble Servt

Go: Washington

NOTES

A NOTE ON SPELLING

1 Christopher Dobbs, "Noah Webster and the Dream of a Common Language," ConnecticutHistory.org, https://connecticuthistory .org/noah-webster-and-the-dream-of-a-common-language/.

INTRODUCTION: WASHINGTON'S GREENHOUSE

1 George Washington, *The Daily Journal of Major George Washington, in 1751–52*, edited by J. M. Toner (Albany, NY: John Munsell's Sons, 1892), p. 58.

2 Mary V. Thompson, "Pineapples," Mount Vernon Digital Encyclopedia, http://www.mountvernon.org/digital-encyclopedia /article/pineapples/.

3 H. S. Paris and J. Janick, "What the Roman Emperor Tiberius Grew in His Greenhouses," Paper, Proceedings of the 9th EUCARPIA meeting on genetics and breeding of Cucurbitaceae, Avignon, France, May 21–24, 2008, available at https://hort .purdue.edu/newcrop/2_13_Janick.pdf.

4 "Way Back When: A History of the English Glasshouse," *Hartley Magazine*, September 3, 2015, https://hartley-botanic.co.uk /magazine/a-history-of-the-english-glasshouse/.

5 Ibid.

6 Mac Griswold, *Washington's Gardens at Mount Vernon: Landscape of the Inner Man* (Boston: Houghton Mifflin, 1999), pp. 94–95.

7 "Greenhouse Gurus," Ohio State University, accessed on March

25, 2018, https://u.osu.edu/greenhousegurus/background -research/history/; Liberty Hyde Bailey, *The Standard Cyclopedia of Horticulture*, second edition (New York: Macmillan Company, 1917), p. 1516, Google Books.

8 "Persecution of Catholics," The Pluralism Project at Harvard University, http://pluralism.org/document/persecution-of -catholics/.

9 Letter from Charles Carroll to George Washington, March 3, 1775, available at https://www.loc.gov/resource/mgw4.033 _0482_0483/?sp=1&st=text.

10 Letter from George Washington to Tench Tilghman, August 11, 1784, available at https://founders.archives.gov/documents /Washington/04-02-02-0032.

11 Letter from George Washington to Margaret Carroll, September 16, 1789, available at https://founders.archives.gov /documents/Washington/05-04-02-0025.

12 Joseph J. Ellis, *His Excellency: George Washington* (New York: Alfred A. Knopf, 2004), pp. 191–192.

13 Letter from Otho Williams to George Washington, October 29, 1789, excerpt available at https://founders.archives.gov /documents/Washington/05-04-02-0025.

14 "The Four Gardens at Mount Vernon," George Washington's Mount Vernon, https://www.mountvernon.org/the-estate -gardens/gardens-landscapes/four-gardens-at-mount-vernon/.

15 Mount Vernon Ladies' Association of the Union, 1916 Annual Report, p. 10, Google Books.

16 Allan Greenberg, *George Washington, Architect* (Berkshire, UK: Andreas Papadakis, 1999), p. 78, Google Books.

17 Harlow Giles Unger, *The Unexpected George Washington* (Hoboken, NJ: John Wiley & Sons, 2006), p. 2.

18 Edward G. Lengel, *First Entrepreneur—How George Washington Built His—and the Nation's—Prosperity* (Boston: Da Capo Press, 2016), p. 4.

19 Kevin J. Hayes, *George Washington: A Life in Books* (New York: Oxford University Press, 2017), p. 103.

20 Quoted in John Berlau, "Recounting George Washington's Brilliant Entrepreneurship," Real Clear Markets, February 22, 2012, http://www.realclearmarkets.com/articles/2012/02/22 /recounting_george_washingtons_brilliant_entrepreneurship _99526.html.

21 Statistics from "Farming the River" exhibit at Donald W. Reynolds Museum and Education Center at George Washington's Mount Vernon.
22 David Humphreys, *Life of General Washington*, edited and with an introduction by Rosemarie Zagarri (Athens, GA: University of Georgia Press, 1991), p. 35.
23 Ibid., p. 36.
24 Paul Johnson, *George Washington: The Founding Father* (New York: HarperCollins/Atlas, 2005), pp. 2–3.
25 Ibid.

CHAPTER 1: IRON ROOTS

1 Johnson, *George Washington*, pp. 2–3.
2 Willard Sterne Randall, *George Washington: A Life* (New York: Henry Holt & Co., 1997), pp. 9–10.
3 Ibid.
4 Ron Chernow, *Washington: A Life* (New York: Penguin Press, 2010), p. 3; Lengel, *First Entrepreneur*, p. 8.
5 Chernow, *Washington*, pp. 3–4.
6 Lengel, *First Entrepreneur*, p. 8.
7 Ibid., p. 9.
8 John Smith, *Travels and Works of Captain John Smith, President of Virginia, and Admiral of New England, 1580–1631*, edited by Edward Arber (New York: Burt Franklin, 1910), pp. 5–40, available at https://www.encyclopediavirginia.org/A_True_relation_of_such_occurrences_and_accidents_of_note_as_hath_hapned_at_Virginia_since_the_first_planting_of_that_Collonyby_John_Smith_1608; Christopher Geist, "The Works at Falling Creek," *Colonial Williamsburg Journal*, fall 2007, https://www.history.org/Foundation/journal/Autumn07/iron.cfm.
9 Sven-Erik Åström, "Swedish Iron and the English Iron Industry About 1700: Some Neglected Aspects," *Scandinavian Economic History Review*, vol. 30, no. 2 (1982), pp. 129–141, Taylor & Francis Online, https://www.tandfonline.com/doi/pdf/10.1080/03585522.1982.10407976?needAccess=true.
10 Lengel, *First Entrepreneur*, pp. 10–11.
11 "Industries: Iron," Stafford County Museum, http://staffordcountymuseum.com/wp-content/uploads/2013/11/Industries-Iron-Mining.pdf.

12 Randall, *George Washington*, p. 238.

13 "Growth of Mount Vernon," Mount Vernon Digital Encyclopedia, https://www.mountvernon.org/library/digitalhistory/digital-encyclopedia/article/growth-of-mount-vernon/.

CHAPTER 2: THE EDUCATION OF AN ENTREPRENEUR

1 Woodrow Wilson, *George Washington* (1896; reprint, New York: Frederick Ungar Publishing Co., 1963), p. 105.

2 Ibid.

3 James Thomas Flexner, *George Washington: The Forge of Experience* (Boston: Little, Brown and Co., 1965), pp. 13–14.

4 Ibid., p. 14.

5 "The Washington House at Ferry Farm," George Washington Foundation, accessed online June 23, 2018, http://www.kenmore.org/ferryfarm/archaeology/wash_house.html.

6 Washington Irving, *Life of George Washington*, vol. 1, in *The Works of Washington Irving* (New York: G.P. Putnam's Sons, 1881), vol. 10, p. 21, Google Books; Harold I. Gullan, *Cradles of Power: The Mothers and Fathers of the American Presidents* (New York: Skyhorse Publishing, 2016), Google Books.

7 Flexner, *George Washington*, pp. 18–19.

8 Ibid., p. 24.

9 Randall, *George Washington*, p. 17.

10 Hayes, *George Washington*, pp. 16–17.

11 Ibid., pp. 7–8.

12 Taylor Soja, "Mary Ball Washington," Mount Vernon Digital Encyclopedia, http://www.mountvernon.org/digital-encyclopedia/article/mary-ball-washington/.

13 Ron Chernow, *Washington* (New York: Penguin Press, 2010), p. 6.

14 Hayes, *George Washington*, p. 9.

15 Hayes uses Mary Washington's signature in copies of books as evidence that she owned and likely read them.

16 Hayes, *George Washington*, pp. 9–10.

17 Ibid., p. 15.

18 Arithmetic was spelled "arithmetick" in the original, reflecting the eighteenth-century spelling.

19 Hayes, *George Washington*, pp. 27–28.

20 Ibid., p. 27.

21 Nina Strochlich, "The Letter That Won the American Rev-

olution," *National Geographic*, July 3, 2017, http://news
.nationalgeographic.com/2017/07/george-washington-spy
-letter/.

22 John Seller, *Practical navigation; or an introduction to the whole art,
containing the doctrine of plain and spherical triangles* (Chicago:
Gale ECCO, 2010).

23 Edward Redmond, "Washington as Public Land Surveyor," Library of Congress, https://www.loc.gov/collections/george
-washington-papers/articles-and-essays/george-washington
-survey-and-mapmaker/washington-as-public-land-surveyor/.

24 Rebecca Onion, "George Washington: Lifelong Mapmaker,"
Slate, February 15, 2016, http://www.slate.com/blogs/the
_vault/2016/02/15/maps_made_by_george_washington_long
time_surveyor_and_cartographer.html.

25 Letter from George Washington to the Continental Congress
Committee to Inquire into the State of the Army, July 19, 1777,
available at https://founders.archives.gov/?q=seldom%20
comes%20within%20the%20verge%20of%20the%20Camp&s
=1111311111&r=1.

26 Ibid., footnote 8.

27 Lola Cazier, *Surveys and Surveyors of the Public Domain 1785–1975*
(Washington, DC: U.S. Government Printing Office, 1975),
pp. 13–14, available online at https://www.ntc.blm.gov/krc
/uploads/538/Sur_Sur_Pub_Dom.pdf.

28 Randall, *George Washington*, pp. 37–38.

29 Martha Saxton, *The Widow Washington: The Life of Mary Washington* (New York: Farrar, Straus and Giroux, 2019), p. 151.

30 Randall, *George Washington*, p. 39.

31 Hayes, *George Washington*, pp. 32–33.

32 Ibid., p. 38.

33 Ibid., pp. 39–41.

34 Since George Washington's lifetime, there has been rampant
speculation of a romantic relationship—and possibly sexual
intercourse—between Washington and Sally Fairfax. His letters to Sally show he was clearly enamored with her, and some
also argue he loved her more than his wife Martha. This book
is concerned with Washington's entrepreneurship and will not
delve into speculation about his love life, except to note that
much more of George's letters to Sally survive, since Martha
burned the letters between George and herself. So although

the few letters between George and Martha seem very tender, there is still much we don't know about the extent of romance between them. See Brigid Schulte, "Fresh Look at Martha Washington: Less First Frump, More Foxy Lady," *Washington Post,* February 2, 2009, p. A1, http://www.washingtonpost.com/wp -dyn/content/story/2009/02/02/ST2009020201419.html.

CHAPTER 3: A DIRTY JOB

1 Donald A. Wise, "The Young Washington as Surveyor," *Northern Virginia Heritage,* October 1979, p. 11.
2 Flexner, *George Washington,* pp. 35–36.
3 Ibid., p. 36.
4 Wise, "The Young Washington as Surveyor," p. 12.
5 Randall, *George Washington,* p. 46.
6 Hayes, *George Washington,* p. 30.
7 William Seale, *A Guide to Historic Alexandria* (Alexandria, VA: The City of Alexandria 250th Anniversary Commission, 2000), p. 20.
8 Lengel, *First Entrepreneur,* p. 21.
9 Stephen Brumwell, *George Washington: Gentleman Warrior* (New York: Quercus, 2012), p. 32.
10 Chernow, *Washington,* p. 23.
11 Flexner, *George Washington,* pp. 38–39.
12 Paul Leland Haworth, *George Washington: Farmer* (Indianapolis: Bobbs-Merrill, 1915), p. 9; Lengel, *First Entrepreneur,* pp. 21–22.
13 Mary Wigge, "Washington's Lease Terms at Mount Vernon," Washington Papers, March 20, 2015, https://gwpapers.virginia .edu/documents/washingtons-lease-terms-at-mount-vernon /; Wilma A. Dunaway, *The First American Frontier: Transition to Capitalism in Southern Appalachia, 1700–1860* (Chapel Hill, NC: University of North Carolina Press, 1996), Google Books.
14 Flexner, *George Washington,* pp. 38–39.
15 Lengel, *First Entrepreneur,* p. 21.
16 Richard Morrison, "Can You Make a Living Without a Government License?" Competitive Enterprise Institute Blog, August 4, 2017, https://cei.org/blog/can-you-make-living-without -government-license.
17 Lengel, *First Entrepreneur,* p. 25.
18 Chernow, *Washington,* p. 32.
19 Ibid., p. 19.

CHAPTER 4: WASHINGTON'S SOCIAL NETWORK

1 Letter from George Washington to Andrew Lewis, March 27, 1775, available at https://founders.archives.gov/documents /Washington/02-10-02-0238.

2 George Washington, "Last Will and Testament," in *The Writings of George Washington,* ed. Worthington Chauncey Ford, vol. 14 (New York: G.P. Putnam's Sons, 1893), p. 302, reprinted at Online Library of Liberty, https://oll.libertyfund.org/titles/washington -the-writings-of-george-washington-vol-xiv-1798-1799.

3 Thomas Paine, "The Cause of the Yellow Fever," in *The Writings of Thomas Paine,* ed. Moncure Daniel Conway, vol. 4 (New York: Knickerbocker Press, 1908), pp. 470–474, Google Books.

4 Taylor Kuykendall, "The History of Natural Gas in West Virginia," *The Register-Herald,* February 23, 2011, https://www.register -herald.com/archives/the-history-of-natural-gas-in-west-virginia /article_94cc77c1-7035-5491-b73f-753ff43123ba.html.

5 Jett Conner, "Rocky Hill Experiment," Mount Vernon Digital Encyclopedia, http://www.mountvernon.org/digital-encyclopedia /article/rocky-hill-experiment/.

6 Doug Everleigh, "George Washington, Scientist," *Chemical & Engineering News,* vol. 92, no. 28 (September 22, 2014), https:// cen.acs.org/articles/92/i38/George-Washington-Scientist .html.

7 "Colonial Manners," Colonial Williamsburg Foundation, http://www.history.org/almanack/life/manners/rules2.cfm.

8 Lengel, *First Entrepreneur,* p. 28.

9 Alexander Immekus, "Freemasonry," Mount Vernon Digital Encyclopedia, http://www.mountvernon.org/digital-encyclopedia /article/freemasonry/.

10 "Rudyard Kipling and His Masonic Career," Pietre-Stones Review of Freemasonry, http://www.freemasons-freemasonry .com/kipling.html.

11 Letter from George Washington to the Masons of Kind David's Lodge, August 18, 1790, available at https://founders.archives .gov/documents/Washington/05-06-02-0136.

12 "Dogs," Mount Vernon Digital Encyclopedia, https://www .mountvernon.org/library/digitalhistory/digital-encyclopedia /article/dogs/; Mary V. Thompson, "Donkeys," Mount Vernon Digital Encyclopedia, https://www.mountvernon.org/library /digitalhistory/digital-encyclopedia/article/donkeys/.

13 Lengel, *First Entrepreneur,* pp. 239–240.

14 Letter from Thomas Jefferson to Walter Jones, January 2, 1814, available at https://founders.archives.gov/documents /Jefferson/03-07-02-0052.

15 Frank Cogliano, "Henrietta Liston and George Washington: A Special Relationship," National Library of Scotland, https:// digital.nls.uk/travels-of-henrietta-liston/long-reads/cogliano .html.

16 Richard Brookhiser, *Founding Father: Rediscovering George Washington* (New York: Free Press, 1996), p. 127.

17 Letter from George Washington to John [last name unknown], circa 1749–50, available at https://founders.archives.gov /documents/Washington/02-01-02-0009.

18 Hayes, *George Washington,* p. 24.

19 Humphreys, *Life of General Washington,* pp. 35–36.

20 Ibid., p. 36.

21 Ibid.

22 Gwendolyn K. White, "Arthur Young," Mount Vernon Digital Encyclopedia, https://www.mountvernon.org/library /digitalhistory/digital-encyclopedia/article/arthur-young/.

23 Ibid., p. 172.

24 Thomas Paine, Letter to George Washington, Introduction by Philip Foner, Thomas Paine National Historical Association, http://thomaspaine.org/major-works/letter-to-george -washington.html.

25 Paine, "The Cause of the Yellow Fever," pp. 470–474.

26 Humphreys, *Life of General Washington,* p. 35.

27 Hayes, *George Washington,* p. 259.

28 Ibid.

29 Ibid.

30 Ibid.

31 "Life Portraits of George Washington," George Washington's Mount Vernon, https://www.mountvernon.org/george -washington/artwork/life-portraits-of-george-washington/.

32 Peter Grier, "The (Semi) Secret History of Trump's Andrew Jackson Portrait," *Christian Science Monitor,* February 9, 2017, https:// www.csmonitor.com/USA/Politics/Decoder/2017/0209/The -semi-secret-history-of-Trump-s-Andrew-Jackson-portrait.

33 Ibid.; Elkanah and Winslow Watson, *Men and Times of the Revolution* (New York: Dana and Company, 1856), p. 119, Google Books.

CHAPTER 5: GEORGE AND MARTHA

1 The most influential historian pushing this narrative was James Thomas Flexner in his four-volume biography of George Washington written in the 1960s and '70s. Flexner, who won a Pulitzer Prize for these works, was a pioneering historian in other respects, and I cite him many times in this book on George's Washington's business ventures and family history. But his gossipy suppositions about a purported "love triangle" of Martha, George, and Sally have been discredited by contemporary historians. To a one, today's respected Washington biographers—such as Chernow, Ellis, Lengel, and Hayes—all conclude based on the limited correspondence of George and Martha and observations of their friends that the Washingtons cared deeply for each other. "I retain an unalterable affection for you," he wrote just before he took command of the Continental Army in the Revolutionary War, "which neither time nor distance can change." Letter from George Washington to Martha Washington, June 23, 1775, https://www.mountvernon.org /george-washington/the-man-the-myth/washington-stories/a -love-letter-from-general-washington/. See also Schulte, "Fresh Look at Martha Washington."
2 Schulte, "Fresh Look at Martha Washington."
3 Ibid.
4 Patricia Brady, *Martha Washington: An American Life* (New York: Viking, 2005), p. 20.
5 Ibid., p. 14.
6 Ibid., p. 20.
7 Ibid., pp. 22–23.
8 Ibid., p. 24; Schulte, "Fresh Look at Martha Washington."
9 Brady, *Martha Washington*, p. 25.
10 Ibid.
11 Ibid.
12 Bruce Chadwick, *The General & Mrs. Washington* (Naperville, IL: Sourcebooks, 2007), p. 40.
13 Brady, *Martha Washington*, pp. 29–30.
14 Ibid., p. 31
15 Ibid., p. 32.
16 Ibid., p. 40.
17 Ibid., pp. 35–41.
18 Ibid., pp. 49–50.

19 Ibid., p. 52.

20 Chadwick, *The General & Mrs. Washington*, p. 48.

21 Ibid., pp. 49–50.

22 Brady, *Martha Washington*, p. 53.

23 Ibid.

24 Chadwick, *The General & Mrs. Washington*, p. 51.

25 Ibid.

26 Brady, *Martha Washington*, p. 61.

27 George Washington, *The Journal of Major George Washington*, edited and with an introduction by Paul Royster, DigitalCommons@University of Nebraska-Lincoln, https://digitalcommons.unl.edu/cgi/viewcontent.cgi?article=1033&context=etas.

28 Hayes, *George Washington*, p. 64.

29 "Ten Facts About George Washington and the French & Indian War," George Washington's Mount Vernon, https://www.mountvernon.org/george-washington/french-indian-war/ten-facts-about-george-washington-and-the-french-indian-war/.

30 Susan Svrluga, "After George Washington Died, His Wife Burned Her Letters. Except These," *Washington Post*, April 28, 2015, https://www.washingtonpost.com/news/grade-point/wp/2015/04/28/after-george-washington-died-his-wife-burned-her-letters-except-these/?utm_term=.8c0cb30651ee.

31 Brady, *Martha Washington*, p. 60.

32 Kiera E. Nolan, "Lawrence Washington," Mount Vernon Digital Encyclopedia, http://www.mountvernon.org/digital-encyclopedia/article/lawrence-washington/.

33 Robert Francis Jones, *George Washington: Ordinary Man, Extraordinary Leader* (New York: Fordham University Press, 2002), p. 24.

34 Brady, *Martha Washington*, p. 65.

35 Letter from George Washington to Arthur Young, December 12, 1793, available at https://founders.archives.gov/documents/Washington/05-14-02-0337.

36 "Expansion of Mount Vernon's Mansion," George Washington's Mount Vernon, https://www.mountvernon.org/the-estate-gardens/the-mansion/expansion-of-mount-vernons-mansion/.

37 Ibid.

38 Chadwick, *The General & Mrs. Washington*, p. 56.

39 Brady, *Martha Washington*, p. 71.

40 Chadwick, *The General & Mrs. Washington*, p. 64.

41 Ibid., pp. 64–65.
42 Ibid.
43 Ibid., p. 65.

CHAPTER 6: WASHINGTON'S GREEN THUMB

1 Wilson, *George Washington,* pp. 104–105.
2 Carol Borchert Cadou, "The Style of Martha Washington," Mount Vernon Digital Encyclopedia, http://www.mountvernon.org/digital-encyclopedia/article/the-style-of-martha-washington/.
3 Lengel, *First Entrepreneur,* p. 44.
4 Chadwick, *The General & Mrs. Washington,* p. 79.
5 Lengel, *First Entrepreneur,* p. 44.
6 Sharon Ann Murphy, "Early American Colonists Had a Cash Problem. Here's How They Solved It," *Time,* February 27, 2017, http://time.com/4675303/money-colonial-america-currency-history/.
7 Letter from George Washington to Robert Cary & Company, May 28, 1762, available at https://founders.archives.gov/?q=cary%20fairfax%20Recipient%3A%22Robert%20Cary%20%26%20Company%22&s=1111311111&sa=&r=5&sr=.
8 Sarah Tumwebaze, "Why Farmers Keep Growing Tobacco," *Daily Monitor,* June 5, 2013, http://www.monitor.co.ug/artsculture/Reviews/Why-farmers-keep-growing-tobacco/691232-1872192-8w8ev6z/index.html.
9 George Washington, Invoice to Robert Cary & Company, May 1, 1759, available at https://founders.archives.gov/?q=New%20Principles%20of%20Gardening&s=1111311111&sa=&r=4&sr=; Letter from George Washington to Robert Cary & Company, October 24, 1760, available at https://founders.archives.gov/documents/Washington/02-06-02-0271.
10 Harlow Giles Unger, *The Unexpected George Washington: His Private Life* (Hoboken, NJ: John Wiley & Sons, Inc. 2006), p. 2.
11 Christopher E. Hendricks and J. Edwin Hendricks, "Expanding to the West: Settlement of the Piedmont Region, 1730 to 1775," *Tar Heel Junior Historian,* vol. 34, no. 2 (spring 1995), available at https://www.ncpedia.org/anchor/expanding-west-settlement.
12 Lengel, *First Entrepreneur,* p. 61.
13 "Washington and Wheat," George Washington's Mount Vernon,

http://www.mountvernon.org/george-washington/farming/washington-and-wheat/.

14 Lengel, *First Entrepreneur*, p. 61.

15 Letter from George Washington to Robert Cary & Company, September 20, 1765, available at https://founders.archives.gov/documents/Washington/02-07-02-0252-0001.

16 Ibid.

17 Hayes, *George Washington*, pp. 101–102.

18 John L. Smith, Jr., "The Truth About George Washington and Hemp," *Journal of the American Revolution*, October 6, 2016, https://allthingsliberty.com/2016/10/truth-george-washington-hemp/.

19 Ibid.; Letter from George Washington to William Pearce, February 24, 1794, available at https://founders.archives.gov/documents/Washington/05-15-02-0210. "India hemp" most likely refers to the hemp grown by American Indians, not the overseas British colony that is now a nation.

20 Letter from George Washington to George William Fairfax, June 30, 1785, available at https://founders.archives.gov/documents/Washington/04-03-02-0080.

21 Letter from George Washington to George Augustine Washington, May 27, 1787, available at https://founders.archives.gov/?q=Correspondent%3A%22Washington%2C%20George%22%20Correspondent%3A%22Washington%2C%20George%20Augustine%22&s=1111311111&r=24.

22 Ibid.; "Cornelius McDermott Roe," Mount Vernon Digitial Encyclopedia, https://www.mountvernon.org/library/digitalhistory/digital-encyclopedia/article/cornelius-mcdermott-roe/.

23 George Washington, diary entry, April 14, 1760, https://www.mountvernon.org/plan-your-visit/tours-activities/washington-experimental-farmer/.

24 George Washington, diary entry, May 1, 1760, https://www.mountvernon.org/plan-your-visit/tours-activities/washington-experimental-farmer/.

25 Letter from George Washington to William Pearce, June 5, 1796, available at https://founders.archives.gov/?q=june%205%2C%201796%20Dates-From%3A1796-06-05&s=1111311111&sa=&r=5&sr=.

26 Letter from Thomas Jefferson to George Washington, June 28, 1793, available at https://founders.archives.gov/documents/Jefferson/01-26-02-0360.

27 Haworth, *George Washington*, p. 53.

28 Letter from George Washington to Arthur Young, December 5, 1791, http://teachingamericanhistory.org/library/document/letter-to-arthur-young/.

29 Aaron Sidder, "The Green, Brown, and Beautiful Story of Compost," *National Geographic*, September 9, 2016, https://www.nationalgeographic.com/people-and-culture/food/the-plate/2016/09/compost—a-history-in-green-and-brown/.

30 Hugh Hammond Bennett, "Soil Erosion a Costly Farm Evil," speech, January 31, 1933, Columbus, Ohio, https://www.nrcs.usda.gov/wps/portal/nrcs/detail/national/about/history/?cid=nrcs143_021397.

31 Natasha Geiling, "The Real Johnny Appleseed Brought Apples—and Booze—to the American Frontier," *Smithsonian*, November 10, 2014, http://www.smithsonianmag.com/arts-culture/real-johnny-appleseed-brought-applesand-booze-american-frontier-180953263/#ucwVoQXxiJV0ClLD.99.

32 Joseph Manca, *George Washington's Eye: Landscape, Architecture, and Design at Mount Vernon* (Baltimore: The Johns Hopkins University Press, 2012), Google Books.

33 "Sugar Maple," George Washington's Mount Vernon, http://www.mountvernon.org/the-estate-gardens/gardens-landscapes/plant-finder/item/sugar-maple/.

34 "Ten Facts About the Gardens at Mount Vernon," George Washington's Mount Vernon, http://www.mountvernon.org/the-estate-gardens/gardens-landscapes/ten-facts-about-the-gardens-at-mount-vernon/.

35 Ibid.

36 "The Four Gardens at Mount Vernon," George Washington's Mount Vernon, http://www.mountvernon.org/the-estate-gardens/gardens-landscapes/four-gardens-at-mount-vernon/.

37 Letter from George Washington to Lund Washington, August 19, 1776, available at https://founders.archives.gov/documents/Washington/03-06-02-0078.

CHAPTER 7: WASHINGTON'S MOUNT VERNON

 1 Mary V. Thompson, "George Washington and Entertainment," Mount Vernon Digital Encyclopedia, http://www.mountvernon.org/digital-encyclopedia/article/george-washington-and-entertainment/#2.

2 Ibid.

3 Ibid.

4 Doug Baum, "The Status of the Camel in the United States of America," paper presented at the Camel Conference @SOAS University of London, May 23–25, 2011, https://www.soas.ac.uk/camelconference2011/file84331.pdf.

5 Kristi King, "Mount Vernon's Christmas Camel a Reminder of Holiday in History," WTOP, December 11, 2014, https://wtop.com/news/2014/12/mount-vernons-christmas-camel-a-reminder-of-holiday-in-history-photos/slide/1/.

6 John Durant, "Virginia's Finest Horseman," *Sports Illustrated*, July 2, 1956, https://www.si.com/vault/1956/07/02/582240/virginias-finest-horseman.

7 Lengel, *First Entrepreneur*, p. 42.

8 James Thomas Flexner, *Washington: The Indispensable Man* (Boston: Little, Brown and Co., 1974), Google Books.

9 Rebekah L. Holt, "George Washington: The All-American Equestrian," eQuest for Truth, http://www.equest4truth.com/component/content/article/94-discover-equus/166-george-washington-the-all-american-equestrian.

10 Lengel, *First Entrepreneur*, p. 157.

11 Alex Probus, "President George Washington's Kentucky Land," *The Kentucky Pioneer*, vol. 11, no. 1 (February 2015), p. 2, http://www.kyssar.org/wordpress1/wp-content/uploads/2015/02/kypioneer-v11-1.pdf.

12 Hayes, *George Washington*, pp. 97–98.

13 Lengel, *First Entrepreneur*, p. 143.

14 Ibid., p. 147.

15 Feather Schwartz Foster, "George Washington: An All-American Uncle," Presidential History Blog, November 30, 2013, https://featherfoster.wordpress.com/2013/11/30/george-washington-an-all-american-uncle/.

16 Stanley Coran, "George Washington: President, General and Dog Breeder," *Psychology Today*, January 2, 2009, https://www.psychologytoday.com/blog/canine-corner/200901/george-washington-president-general-and-dog-breeder.

17 "Independence Day Special: Revolutionary Hound Dogs," American Kennel Club History & Archive, October 14, 2014, http://www.akc.org/content/akc-history-archive/articles/independence-day-special-george-washington/.

18 Randall, *George Washington*, p. 414.

19 Ibid.; Johanna Bakmas, "Royal Gift (Donkey)," http://www
.mountvernon.org/digital-encyclopedia/article/royal-gift
-donkey/.

20 Bakmas, "Royal Gift (Donkey)."

21 Ibid.

22 Angela Jane Howard, "The Royal Jack and the Knight of
Malta," The Receding Landscape, November 20, 2016, http://
angelajanehoward.com/en/the-royal-jack-and-the-knight-of
-malta/.

23 Marye Roser, "Commercial Mule Packing in the Sierra," Mule
Museum, http://www.mulemuseum.org/commercial-packing
.html.

24 Ibid., pp. 62–63.

25 "Ten Facts About the Gristmill," George Washington's Mount
Vernon, http://www.mountvernon.org/the-estate-gardens/grist
mill/ten-facts-about-the-gristmill/.

26 Lengel, *First Entrepreneur*, p. 63.

27 Ibid., p. 64.

28 "Ten Facts About the Gristmill."

29 Lengel, *First Entrepreneur*, p. 64.

30 Ibid.

31 George Washington, diary entry, April 3, 1772, available at
https://founders.archives.gov/documents/Washington/01
-03-02-0002-0008-0003.

32 George Washington, diary entry, December 22, 1772, available at https://founders.archives.gov/?q=%22g%20washing-
ton%22%20flour&s=1111311111&sa=&r=4&sr=.

33 In 1845, New York became the first state to pass a trademark protection law. About a dozen states followed over the next 25 years.
Stuart Banner, *American Property* (Cambridge, MA: Harvard University Press, 2011), p. 30. In 1870, the U.S. Congress put provisions protecting trademarks into the Copyright Acts. However,
the Supreme Court struck down these provisions as exceeding
Congress' powers under the patent and copyright clause of the
Constitution, as the court argued that "a trade-mark is neither
an invention, a discovery, nor a writing." But the Trademark Act
of 1881, which was based on Congress' power under the Constitution to regulate interstate commerce, survived constitutional
scrutiny. *Trademark Cases*, 100 U.S. 82 (1879).

34 "Some Well-Known U.S. Trademarks Celebrate One Hundred Years," United States Patent and Trademark Office, Press Release #00-38, June 15, 2000, https://www.uspto.gov/about-us /news-updates/some-well-known-us-trademarks-celebrate-one -hundred-years.

35 Richard Tedlow, *New and Improved: The Story of Mass Marketing in America* (New York: Basic Books, 1990), p. 14, quoted in Nancy F. Koehn, "Henry Heinz and Brand Creation in the Late Nineteenth Century: Making Markets for Processed Food," *Business History Review*, vol. 73, no. 3 (autumn 1999), https://www.cambridge.org/core/journals/business-history -review/article/henry-heinz-and-brand-creation-in-the-late -nineteenth-century-making-markets-for-processed-food/ED3 AA32FE1989296B27D1782A5BD27E7.

36 Ron Chernow, *Alexander Hamilton* (New York: Penguin, 2004), Google Books.

37 Lee Brodie, "George Washington Could Have Held This Stock," CNBC, February 18, 2013, https://www.cnbc.com/id /100464817.

38 Alexa Price, "Mount Vernon Fisheries," Mount Vernon Digital Encyclopedia, https://www.mountvernon.org/library/digital history/digital-encyclopedia/article/mount-vernon-fisheries/.

39 "George Washington's Fisheries," George Washington's Mount Vernon, http://www.mountvernon.org/the-estate-gardens/historic -trades/fisheries/.

40 S. Fiona Bessey and Dennis J. Pogue, "Blacksmithing at George Washington's Mount Vernon," Mount Vernon Digital Collection, pp. 176–185.

41 Ibid.

CHAPTER 8: SUCCESS AND REVOLUTION

1 Donald N. Moran, "Why George Washington?" Revolutionary Archives, http://www.revolutionarywararchives.org /washwhyhim.html.

2 John Adams, *Diary of John Adams*, "In Congress, June and July 1775," available at http://founders.archives.gov/documents /Adams/01-03-02-0016-0025.

3 Michael Schellhammer, "Wondering About Washington," *Journal of the American Revolution*, January 15, 2013, https:// allthingsliberty.com/2013/01/wondering-about-washington/.

4 "Salt Preservation," George Washington's Mount Vernon, http://www.mountvernon.org/the-estate-gardens/historic -trades/fisheries/salt-preservation/.

5 Thomas Jefferson, *The Writings of Thomas Jefferson: 1781–1784*, edited by Paul Leicester Ford, vol. 3 (New York: G.P. Putnam's Sons, 1894), pp. 113–114, Google Books.

6 "The Iron Act (1750)," Alpha History, https://alphahistory .com/americanrevolution/iron-act-1750/.

7 Ibid.

8 "Hat Act," Revolvy, https://www.revolvy.com/page/Hat-Act.

9 "Wool Act 1699," Revolvy, https://www.revolvy.com/page/Wool -Act-1699.

10 Lyman Horace Weeks, *A History of Paper-Manufacturing in the United States, 1690–1916* (New York: Lockwood, 1916), p. 41, Google Books.

11 Ibid., p. 93; Maria Mihalik Higgins, *Benjamin Franklin: Revolutionary Inventor* (New York: Sterling, 2007), p. 59, Google Books.

12 Weeks, *A History of Paper-Manufacturing in the United States, 1690–1916*, pp. 42–43.

13 Johnson, *George Washington*, p. 55.

14 Edmund S. Morgan and Helen S. Morgan, *The Stamp Act Crisis: Prologue to Revolution* (Chapel Hill, NC: University of North Carolina Press, 2011), p. 72, Google Books.

15 Woody Holton, *Forced Founders: Indians, Debtors, Slaves, and the Making of the American Revolution in Virginia* (Chapel Hill, NC: University of North Carolina Press, 1999), p. 56.

16 Ibid., p. 210.

17 Carl G. Karsch, "My Zeal for Liberty," Carpenters' Hall, http:// www.ushistory.org/carpentershall/history/zeal.htm.

18 Letter from Charles Thomson—"A Merchant in Philadelphia"—to Benjamin Franklin, June 19, 1765, available at https://founders.archives.gov/documents/Franklin/01-12-02 -0088; see notes on letter writer's identity.

19 Ibid.

20 Flexner, *George Washington*, p. 312.

21 Letter from George Washington to George Mason, April 5, 1769, available at http://www.loc.gov/teachers/classroommaterials /presentationsandactivities/presentations/timeline/amrev /brittwo/mason.html.

22 John Dickinson, "Letter 2—Letters from a Farmer in Pennsylvania," *Pennsylvania Gazette*, December 10, 1767, http://americainclass.org/sources/makingrevolution/crisis/text4/dickinsonletters1767.pdf.

23 Ibid.

24 Holton, *Forced Founders*, pp. 57–58.

25 Chadwick, *The General & Mrs. Washington*, p. 96.

26 Memo from Mary V. Thompson, March 11, 2002, George Washington's Mount Vernon.

27 Ibid.; Mary V. Thompson, "Sheep," Mount Vernon Digital Encyclopedia, https://www.mountvernon.org/library/digitalhistory/digital-encyclopedia/article/sheep/; Letter from George Washington to John Sinclair, July 20, 1794, available at https://founders.archives.gov/documents/Washington/05-16-02-0311.

28 Memo from Mary V. Thompson.

29 Erin Allen and Julie Miller, "George Washington and the Weaving of American History," Library of Congress Blog, March 10, 2015, https://blogs.loc.gov/loc/2015/03/george-washington-and-the-weaving-of-american-history/.

30 Flora Fraser, *The Washingtons: George and Martha* (New York: Alfred A. Knopf, 2015).

31 All quotations from the Fairfax Resolves are from "Fairfax Resolves," July 18, 1774, Gunston Hall, http://www.gunstonhall.org/georgemason/human_rights/fairfax_resolves.html.

32 See Iain McLean and Scot M. Peterson, "Adam Smith at the Constitutional Convention," *Loyola Law Review*, vol. 56 (June 17, 2010), pp. 95–133, http://law.loyno.edu/sites/law.loyno.edu/files/McLean-Peterson-FI-PSL.pdf.

33 George Washington, "First Inaugural Address: Final Version," April 30, 1789, available at https://founders.archives.gov/?q=%22invisible%20hand%22&s=1111311111&sa=&r=1&sr=.

34 Ibid.; Adam Smith, *The Theory of Moral Sentiments and Essays on Philosophical Subjects* (London: Alex. Murray & Son, 1869), p. 207, reprinted at Online Library of Liberty, https://oll.libertyfund.org/titles/theory-of-moral-sentiments-and-essays-on-philosophical-subjects.

35 Washington, "First Inaugural Address"; Smith, *The Theory of Moral Sentiments and Essays on Philosophical Subjects*, p. 163.

36 Samuel Fleischacker, "Adam Smith's Reception Among the American Founders, 1776–1790," History Cooperative, https://

historycooperative.org/journal/adam-smiths-reception-among
-the-american-founders-1776-1790/.

37 See Charles A. Beard, *An Economic Interpretation of the Constitution of the United States* (New York: Macmillan Company, 1921). Beard was writing primarily of the motives of the signers of the U.S. Constitution. Those writers he influenced would expand the argument to assert that support for the American Revolution in its entirety was primarily about preserving wealth. See Howard Zinn, *A People's History of the United States* (London: Longman Group, 1980). For a stinging critique of Zinn's scholarship by a liberal academic, read David Greenberg, "Agit-Prof," *New Republic*, March 19, 2013, https://newrepublic.com/article/112574/howard-zinns-influential-mutilations-american-history.

38 See Forrest McDonald, *We the People: The Economic Origins of the Constitution*, revised edition (London: Routledge, 1991); see Gordon S. Wood, *The Creation of the American Republic, 1776–1787* (Chapel Hill, NC: University of North Carolina Press; London: Oxford University Press, 1969).

39 Lengel, *First Entrepreneur*, p. 87.

40 Fraser, *The Washingtons*, pp. 243–244.

CHAPTER 9: FATHER OF INVENTION

1 Lengel, *First Entrepreneur*, p. 1.

2 Ibid., pp. 1–3.

3 Ibid., p. 3.

4 Letter from Thomas Jefferson to Walter Jones, January 2, 1814, available at https://founders.archives.gov/documents/Jefferson/03-07-02-0052.

5 Letter from George Washington to Louis Lebègue Duportail, April 4, 1784, in *The Writings of George Washington*, (Boston: Little, Brown and Co., 1858), pp. 36–37.

6 Andrea Sutcliffe, *Steam: The Untold Story of America's First Great Invention* (New York: St. Martin's Press, 2015), quoted in John Berlau, "How George Washington Propelled Steamboats, America's First Great Disruptive Technology," *Forbes*, February 11, 2016, https://www.forbes.com/sites/johnberlau/2016/02/11/how-george-washington-propelled-steamboats-americas-first-great-disruptive-technology/#7725f5d2f9c4.

7 Quoted in J. M. Toner, *George Washington as an Inventor and*

Promoter of the Useful Arts (Washington, DC: Gedney & Roberts Press, 1892), p. 8, Google Books.

8 United States Constitution, Article 1, Section 8, Clause 8, https://constitutioncenter.org/interactive-constitution.

9 Toner, *George Washington as an Inventor and Promoter of the Useful Arts*, pp. 7–8.

10 Ibid., pp. 60–61.

11 "Farming Inventions of George Washington," *Modern Mechanix*, March 1932, p. 75, http://blog.modernmechanix.com/farming -inventions-of-george-washington/; Patrick McGuire, "America's 'First Farmer': The Farming Practices of George Washington," paper, p. 4, available at http://citeseerx.ist.psu.edu/viewdoc /download?doi=10.1.1.583.8535&rep=rep1&type=pdf.

12 Haworth, *George Washington*, pp. 125–127.

13 Joel Achenbach, *The Grand Idea: George Washington's Potomac and the Race to the West* (New York: Simon & Schuster, 2005), pp. 144–150.

14 Ibid., p. 47.

15 Ibid.

16 Ibid., pp. 27–28.

17 Sutcliffe, *Steam*.

18 Letter from James Madison to Thomas Jefferson, January 9, 1785, available at https://founders.archives.gov/documents /Jefferson/01-07-02-0433.

19 Chernow, *Washington*, p. 480.

20 Lengel, *First Entrepreneur*, p. 171.

21 Brookhiser, *Founding Father*, p. 49.

22 Sutcliffe, *Steam*.

23 Ibid.

24 Rand Simberg, *Safe Is Not an Option: Overcoming the Futile Obsession with Getting Everyone Back Alive That Is Killing Our Expansion into Space* (New York: Interglobal Media LLC, 2014), quoted in John Berlau, "How George Washington Propelled Steamboats, America's First Great Disruptive Technology," *Forbes*, February 11, 2016, https://www.forbes.com/sites/johnberlau/2016/02 /11/how-george-washington-propelled-steamboats-americas -first-great-disruptive-technology/#7725f5d2f9c4.

25 James Thomas Flexner, *Steamboats Come True: American Inventors in Action* (New York: Viking Press, 1944), p. 4.

26 Robert O. Woods, "The Genesis of the Steamboat," *Mechani-*

cal Engineering, April 2009, http://www.asme.org/engineering
-topics/articles/history-of-mechanical-engineering/the
-genesis-of-the-steamboat.

27 Tom Ricci, "Robert Fulton," American Society of Mechanical Engineers, May 14, 2012, https://www.asme.org/topics-resources
/content/robert-fulton; Mary Bellis, "The History of Steamboats," ThoughtCo, July 26, 2019, https://www.thoughtco.com
/history-of-steamboats-4057901.

28 Deirdre Nansen McCloskey, "Why Economics Can't Explain
the Modern World," background paper for an address to
the Australian Conference of Economists, Melbourne, Aus-
tralia, July 9, 2012, p. 16, http://www.deirdremccloskey.com
/docs/australia.docx; Deirdre Nansen McCloskey, "The Great
Enrichment," *National Review*, November 19, 2015, http://
www.nationalreview.com/article/426722/great-enrichment
-deirdre-nansen-mccloskey.

29 Deirdre Nansen McCloskey, *Bourgeois Dignity: Why Economics
Can't Explain the Modern World* (Chicago: University of Chicago
Press, 2010), p. 23.

CHAPTER 10: NEVER AT REST

1 Sam Moore, "Oliver Evans' Improved Gristmill," *Farm Collector*,
May 2011, https://www.farmcollector.com/equipment/oliver
-evans-improved-grist-mill.

2 Achenbach, *The Grand Idea*, pp. 144–150.

3 Letter from George Washington to William Pearce, November
23, 1794, available at https://founders.archives.gov/documents
/Washington/05-17-02-0135.

4 Ibid.

5 Esther White, "James Anderson: Washington's Plantation Manager," Those Pre-Pro Whiskey Men, April 7, 2017, http://pre
-prowhiskeymen.blogspot.com/2017/04/james-anderson
-washingtons-plantation.html.

6 Ibid.

7 Dennis J. Pogue and Esther C. White, *George Washington's Gristmill at Mount Vernon* (Mount Vernon, VA: Mount Vernon Ladies
Association, 2005), p. 47.

8 "Ten Facts About the Distillery," George Washington's Mount
Vernon, http://www.mountvernon.org/the-estate-gardens
/distillery/ten-facts-about-the-distillery/.

9 Ibid.

10 Emily Bilski, "Whiskey Production," Mount Vernon Digital En-cyclopedia, http://www.mountvernon.org/digital-encyclopedia /article/whiskey-production/.

11 Julian Niemcewicz, *Under Their Vine and Fig Tree*, trans. Metchie J. E. Budka (Newark: The Grassman Publishing Company, Inc., 1965), p. 100, quoted in "Ten Facts About the Distillery," George Washington's Mount Vernon, http://www.mountvernon.org /the-estate-gardens/distillery/ten-facts-about-the-distillery/.

12 Ibid.

13 Pogue and White, *George Washington's Gristmill at Mount Vernon*, pp. 51–52.

14 Ibid.

15 Lengel, *First Entrepreneur*, p. 241.

16 Fritz Hirschfeld, *George Washington and Slavery: A Documen-tary Portrayal* (Columbia, MO: University of Missouri Press, 1997).

17 Henry Wiencek, *An Imperfect God: George Washington, His Slaves, and the Creation of America* (New York: Farrar, Straus and Giroux, 2003), p. 6.

18 Ibid., pp. 230–231.

19 Brookhiser, *Founding Father*, p. 182.

20 "Slave Labor," Mount Vernon Digital Encyclopedia, http:// www.mountvernon.org/digital-encyclopedia/article/slave -labor/.

21 Letter from George Washington to Alexander Spotswood, No-vember 23, 1794, available at https://founders.archives.gov /documents/Washington/05-17-02-0136.

22 Letter from George Washington to Robert Lewis, August 17, 1799, available at https://founders.archives.gov/documents /Washington/06-04-02-0211.

23 "Ten Facts About Washington and Slavery," George Washing-ton's Mount Vernon, http://www.mountvernon.org/george -washington/slavery/ten-facts-about-washington-slavery/.

24 Letter from George Washington to John Mercer, September 9, 1786, available at https://www.gilderlehrman.org/content /george-washington-abolition-slavery-1786.

25 Letter from George Washington to Arthur Young, June 18–21, 1792, available at https://founders.archives.gov/documents /Washington/05-10-02-0308.

26 Robert F. Dalzell and Lee Baldwin Dalzell, *George Washington's Mount Vernon: At Home in Revolutionary America* (New York: Oxford University Press, 1998), pp. 212–213.

27 Mary V. Thompson, "'The Only Unavoidable Subject of Regret,'" Mount Vernon Digital Encyclopedia, http://www.mountvernon.org/george-washington/slavery/the-only-unavoidable-subject-of-regret/.

28 George Washington, "Last Will and Testament," July 9, 1799, available at https://founders.archives.gov/documents/Washington/06-04-02-0404-0001.

29 Ibid.

30 Ibid.

31 Wiencek, *An Imperfect God*, pp. 355–356.

32 Ibid., pp. 5–6.

33 Washington, "Last Will and Testament."

34 Brookhiser, *Founding Father*, p. 183.

35 Chernow, *Washington: A Life*, p. 802.

CHAPTER 11: MOUNT VERNON AND WASHINGTON'S LEGACY

1 Kate Egner, "Ann Pamela Cunningham," Mount Vernon Digital Encyclopedia, http://www.mountvernon.org/digital-encyclopedia/article/ann-pamela-cunningham/.

2 Ibid.; Matthew Costello, "John Augustine Washington III," Mount Vernon Digital Encyclopedia, http://www.mountvernon.org/digital-encyclopedia/article/john-augustine-washington-iii/.

3 "Henry Ford to the Rescue," MountVernon.org, http://www.mountvernon.org/preservation/historic-preservation/henry-ford-to-the-rescue/; "Famous Visits to Washington's Tomb," George Washington's Mount Vernon, https://www.mountvernon.org/the-estate-gardens/the-tombs/famous-visits-to-washingtons-tomb/.

4 Telephone interview with Doug Bradburn, November 28, 2017.

5 Mary V. Thompson, "Dining at Mount Vernon," Mount Vernon Digital Encyclopedia, http://www.mountvernon.org/digital-encyclopedia/article/dining-at-mount-vernon/.

6 Search results accessed December 9, 2019, https://www.mountvernon.org/search/?q=debt#gsc.tab=0&gsc.q=debt&gsc.page=1.

7 Michelle Legro, "From Invisible Ink to Cryptography, How the American Revolution Did Spycraft and Privacy-Hacking,"

BrainPicking, https://www.brainpickings.org/2012/02/28/invisible-ink/.

8 "Surveying," Thomas Jefferson Encyclopedia, https://www.monticello.org/site/research-and-collections/surveying.

9 Carl Sandburg, *Abraham Lincoln: The Prairie Years and The War Years* (New York: Harcourt, Brace & Co., 1926), pp. 44–46.

10 Tallia Del Bianco, "Lincoln as a Surveyor," IUPUI.edu, September 1, 2017, https://issuu.com/landsurveyor/docs/lincoln surveyoriconography.

11 Walt Robillard, "The Forgotten Surveyor on the Mountain," January 2014, pp. 21–24, http://www.amerisurv.com/PDF/TheAmericanSurveyor_Robillard-ForgottenSurveyorOnTheMountain_Jan2014.pdf.

12 "Surveying and Mapping Technicians," *Occupational Outlook Handbook*, Bureau of Labor Statistics, https://www.bls.gov/ooh/architecture-and-engineering/surveyors.htm.

13 Ibid., https://www.bls.gov/ooh/architecture-and-engineering/surveyors.htm#tab-4.

14 "Virginia Surveyor Apprenticeship Standards," Virginia Department of Professional and Occupational Regulation, September 14, 2016, https://www.townhall.virginia.gov/L/GetFile.cfm?File=C:%5CTownHall%5Cdocroot%5CGuidanceDocs%5C222%5CGDoc_DPOR_6043_v1.pdf.

15 Tyler Cowen, "The Unseen Threat to America: We Don't Leave Our Hometowns," *Time*, February 22, 2017, http://time.com/4677919/tyler-cowen-book/.

16 Michelle Cottle, "The Onerous, Arbitrary, Unaccountable World of Occupational Licensing," *The Atlantic*, August 13, 2017, https://www.theatlantic.com/politics/archive/2017/08/trump-obama-occupational-licensing/536619/.

17 Clyde Wayne Crews, Jr., "Testimony Before the House Oversight and Government Reform Committee, Subcommittee on Health Care, Benefits, and Administrative Rules, and Subcommittee on Government Operations, Regulatory Reform Task Force Check-In," October 24, 2017, https://oversight.house.gov/wp-content/uploads/2017/10/Wayne-Crews-Regulatory-Reform-Task-Force-Testimony-10242017.pdf.

18 Steve Eder, "When Picking Apples on a Farm with 5,000 Rules, Watch Out for the Ladders," *New York Times*, December 27, 2017, https://www.nytimes.com/2017/12/27/business/picking

-apples-on-a-farm-with-5000-rules-watch-out-for-the-ladders .html.

19 Marisa Manley, "A Victim of Wetland Regulations," Foundation for Economic Education, July 1, 1997, https://fee.org/articles /a-victim-of-wetlands-regulations/.

20 *Securities and Exchange Commission v. W. J. Howey Co.*, 328 U.S. 293, 1946, http://caselaw.findlaw.com/us-supreme-court/328 /293.html.

21 Michael Del Castillo, "A 'Howey Test' for Blockchain? Why the SEC's ICO Guidance Isn't Enough," CoinDesk, August 6, 2017, https://www.coindesk.com/every-token-snowflake-secs -ico-guidance-isnt-enough/; John Berlau, "Cryptocurrency and the SEC's Limitless Power Grab," *OnPoint*, No. 253, April 11, 2019, https://cei.org/sites/default/files/John_Berlau_ -_Cryptocurrency_and_the_SEC_s_Limitless_Power_Grab.pdf.

22 George Washington, "Farewell Address to the People of the United States," September 19, 1796, pp. 18–19, available at https://www.gpo.gov/fdsys/pkg/GPO-CDOC-106sdoc21/pdf /GPO-CDOC-106sdoc21.pdf.

23 Ryan Young, "Congress Should Use REINS Act to Reform Regulation," Competitive Enterprise Institute Blog, November 15, 2016, https://cei.org/blog/congress-should-use-reins-act -reform-regulation.

24 See Peter J. Wallison, *Judicial Fortitude: The Last Chance to Rein in the Administrative State* (New York: Encounter Books, 2018).

APPENDIX

1 Brookhiser, *Founding Father*, p. 192.

2 Flexner, *George Washington*, p. 312.

INDEX